SHRM
Q&A
SERIES

D1536741

Frequently Asked Questions About Staffing Management

SHRM
Q&A
SERIES

Frequently Asked Questions About Staffing Management

with Answers from

SHRM's Knowledge Advisors

Edited by Margaret Fiester, SHRM-SCP

Society for Human Resource
Management
Alexandria, Virginia
shrm.org

Society for Human Resource
Management
Haidian District Beijing, China
shrm.org/cn

Strategic Human Resource
Management India
Mumbai, India
shrmindia.org

Society for Human Resource
Management, Middle East
and Africa Office
Dubai, UAE
shrm.org/pages/mena.aspx

SHRM Q&A Series

107 Frequently Asked Questions
About Staffing Management:
with Answers from SHRM's Knowledge Advisors

47 Frequently Asked Questions
About the Family and Medical Leave Act:
with Answers from SHRM's Knowledge Advisors

57 Frequently Asked Questions
About Workplace Safety and Security:
with Answers from SHRM's Knowledge Advisors

97 Frequently Asked Questions
About Compensation:
with Answers from SHRM's Knowledge Advisors

Founded in 1948, the Society for Human Resource Management (SHRM) is the world's largest HR membership organization devoted to human resource management. Representing more than 275,000 members in over 160 countries, the Society is the leading provider of resources to serve the needs of HR professionals and advance the professional practice of human resource management. SHRM has more than 575 affiliated chapters within the United States and subsidiary offices in China, India, and United Arab Emirates. Visit SHRM Online at www.shrm.org.

Interior and Cover Design: Shirley E.M. Raybuck

Library of Congress Cataloging-in-Publication Data

104 frequently asked questions about staffing management : with answers from SHRM's knowledge advisors / edited by Margaret Fiester, SHRM-SCP.

pages cm. -- (SHRM Q&A series)

Includes bibliographical references and index.

ISBN 978-1-58644-373-3 (alk. paper)

1. Employees--Recruiting. 2. Personnel management. 3. Employee selection. 4. Affirmative action programs. I. Fiester, Margaret. II. Title: One hundred four frequently asked questions about staffing management. III. Title: One hundred and four frequently asked questions about staffing management.

HF5549.5.R44A14 2014

658.3--dc23

2014023019

14-0555

Contents

Introduction...1

Acknowledgments 3

**Chapter 1. Affirmative Action Programs, the Equal
Employment Opportunity Commission, and the
Office of Federal Contract Compliance Programs..............5**

Q: What are the filing requirements for the EEO-I form?..................5

Q: How should employers report telecommuters and remote
workers on the EEO-1 survey? 6

Q: Should employers collect race and other demographic
data during the application process or after employment
starts?..7

Q: What is an affirmative action program? 8

Q: When would a company need to have an affirmative
action program?..8

Q: Where do employers get demographic data for affirmative
action programs?.. 11

Q: Does the Office of Federal Contract Compliance
Programs' rule on the definition of Internet applicant
mean all electronic submissions of interest are applicants?.... 11

Q: When federal contractors subject to affirmative action
requirements search online resume databases, are the
individuals who submitted the resumes considered
applicants under the Office of Federal Contract
Compliance Programs' rules? 12

Chapter 2. Applicants 17

Q: Should employment applications request an applicant's Social Security number? 17

Q: Should certain questions not appear on an employment application? 17

Q: What are the pros and cons of accepting applications or resumes when an employer has no positions open? 20

Q: Do federal or state laws prohibit employers from asking applicants about arrests and convictions? 22

Q: Can a company have a policy to disqualify applicants who fail drug tests from the possibility of future employment? 23

Q: May an employer ask to see an applicant's prior performance reviews? 25

Q: What accommodations should a company make for applicants with disabilities? 27

Q: Is it illegal to ask for an applicant's or employee's date of birth? 28

Q: How can employers protect themselves from liability when giving references? 29

Q: How should a U.S. employer evaluate a foreign degree? 31

Q: Must all employers check applicants against a terrorist list before hiring? 32

Q: What are the federal record retention guidelines for applications and resumes of candidates who are not selected? 33

Chapter 3. Background Investigations 35

Q: When must employers comply with the Fair Credit Reporting Act? 35

Q: Why should an employer verify an applicant's education? 36

Q: Are there any restrictions when performing background checks or drug tests on minors? 37

Q: What should an employer look for when selecting a background check vendor? 39

Q: Which employees must be processed through E-Verify? Can employers verify all employees?.. 40

Q: When must an employer respond to a verification of employment request, and what information must or can be given? 41

Chapter 4. Drug and Alcohol Testing.................................. 45

Q: Must all companies follow the Fair Credit Reporting Act guidelines for drug tests? 45

Q: What are the requirements for drug testing commercial vehicle operators and employees who drive as part of the job? 46

Chapter 5. Employment Offers 49

Q: Can an employer rescind a job offer? 49

Q: What factors should I consider when determining where to place a new hire within the pay range? 50

Q: When a company hires a new employee, must the new hire be provided with an offer letter? What should be included in an offer letter to avoid the perception of an employment contract? 52

Chapter 6. Hiring Decisions... 55

Q: Are there regulations that require a company to post open positions, either internally or externally? If so, is there a requirement on the length of time for the internal posting? 55

Q: What is the difference between equal employment opportunity, affirmative action, and diversity? What is the difference between disparate impact and disparate treatment?... 56

Q: Are all employers with 15 or more employees required to follow the Uniform Guidelines on Employee Selection Procedures, including adverse impact testing and applicant tracking? 58

Q: May a religious institution give preference to hiring adherents of the same religion? What is a ministerial exception under Title VII? 59

Q: Can a company refuse to hire individuals who smoke? 61

Q: What should an employer tell a candidate who is not selected for the position? 62

Q: What should HR consider when rehiring employees? 63

Chapter 7. Interviewing 65

Q: Can a recruiter ask a candidate, "Do you own a car?" 65

Q: Is there a problem with writing notes directly on applications or resumes? 66

Q: What are some tips for screening resumes? 66

Q: When would an employer use a group interview technique? .. 69

Q: How should an employer interview applicants with disabilities? 70

Chapter 8. Management and Communication 73

Q: When should a worker be classified as part time or full time? 73

Q: What factors should determine how many direct reports a manager has? 74

Q: What are the advantages of cafeteria-style relocation programs? 76

Q: What is an effective practice for announcing new hires? 78

Chapter 9. Pre-employment Testing 79

Q: What compliance issues are involved in creating a pre-employment test? 79

Q: What do we need to do to implement a pre-employment drug screening? 79

Q: What are the compliance issues involved in conducting pre-employment physical examinations? 81

Q: How should a company implement a pre-employment testing program? 81

Chapter 10. Recruiting 85

Q: Can an employer skip the recruiting process, including job posting, if it has already identified a candidate it wants to hire or promote? 85

Q: Can a company advertise for candidates with the requirement that they must be currently employed? 86

Chapter 11. Retention, Turnover, and Onboarding 89

Q: How do I calculate retention? Is retention related to turnover? 89

Q: Are there any positives to turnover? 90

Q: When conducting stay interviews, how can employers mitigate trust issues employees may have with the process?. 92

Q: What is the advantage of a buddy system? 93

Chapter 12. Talent Pool 95

Q: What is sourcing? 95

Q: Our company would like to determine the quality of candidates in a region where we are considering opening a new office. Should we post a job ad for a position that doesn't yet exist? 95

Q: How can sourcing give us a competitive staffing edge? 97

Q: Recruiters are calling and e-mailing our employees at work during business hours. Is this legal? 99

Q: What is a corporate alumni association? 100

Q: Why is it important to recruit from diverse sources? 101

Q: How can a company make the best use of career fairs? 102

Q: Where can I access employers that have had successful experiences hiring people with disabilities? 104

Q: What is an employee referral program? 105

Q: Do employee referral programs negatively affect diversity in the workplace? If so, what should HR professionals do to address the problem? 106

Chapter 13. Temporary Employees, Independent Contractors, and Interns 109

Q: How long can a temporary employee retain temporary status before we have to consider the employee regular? 109

Q: What guidance exists for employers when managing the relationship with an independent contractor? 110

Q: What is a statutory employee? 112

Q: Can interns be independent contractors? 112

Q: Can an independent contractor or consultant manage company employees? 113

Chapter 14. Terminations and Downsizing 115

Q: How often should exit interview results be presented to senior managers? What should be reported? 115

Q: What criteria should be used in selecting employees for layoff? 116

Q: What are "bumping" rights? 118

Q: What is the difference between a furlough, a layoff, and a reduction in force? 119

Q: Can we include employees who have performance problems in a reduction in force? 120

Q: Can an employer terminate and rehire an employee as an independent contractor doing the same job? 121

Q: How long after eliminating a position should we wait before filling a position? 122

Chapter 15. Veterans 125

Q: What is the difference between the VETS 100 and VETS 100A report forms, and who should file each? 125

Q: What is veterans' preference, and is it required in the private sector? 126

Chapter 16. Visas and I-9 Compliance 129

Q: Can a company refuse to consider a candidate who is not eligible to work in the United States and would require sponsorship for an H-1B visa? 129

Q: How do I hire a foreign national to work in the United States? 130

Q: What is an H-1B visa? 131

Q: What must an employer do to obtain an H-1B visa for a potential employee? 132

Q: How should an employer transfer a candidate's H-1B visa from his or her current employer? 133

Q: What is an H-2B certification? 134

Q: How can an employer file an Application for Permanent Employment Certification, ETA Form 9089? 136

Q: What is the foreign labor certification process for hiring foreign workers? 137

Q: What is a permanent labor certification? 137

Q: How does an employer go about sponsoring a worker for a green card? 139

Q: What is an employer's responsibility when an employee with an H-1B visa is terminated? 141

Q: How does NAFTA affect hiring employees from Canada and Mexico? 143

Q: How can an employer prevent the employment of illegal workers? 145

Chapter 17. Workforce Planning and Readiness 149

Q: How does trend analysis fit into workforce planning? 149

Q: How should a company develop a staffing plan? 150

Q: How do I conduct a job analysis to ensure the job description actually matches the duties performed by the employee in the job? 152

Q: How should a downsized organization approach staffing needs? 153

Q: I would like to partner with local colleges to develop a workforce with the skills that our company needs. How can I get started? 155

Chapter 18. Working Conditions 157

Q: Can employers change an employee's job duties, schedule, or work location without his or her consent or prior notification? 157

Q: What factors should employers consider prior to instituting a telecommuting policy? 158

Q: What are some common types of alternative schedules? 161

Q: What are some job and employee characteristics that make a good fit for telecommuting? 162

Q: What are some potential benefits and risks of telecommuting, both for the employer and employee? 163

Q: What is hoteling? 165

Q: What should employers consider when instituting a compressed workweek? 165

Endnotes 167

Index 179

Additional SHRM-Published Books 191

Introduction

This book contains frequently asked questions and answers gathered over the years by the Society for Human Resource Management's HR Knowledge Advisors in response to members' questions on various staffing management-related topics. The book will benefit HR generalists and individuals new to the HR function, who may not be familiar with the best practices, laws, and regulatory compliance related to hiring a workforce.

Acknowledgments

SHRM's HR Knowledge Center is a free service to SHRM members. SHRM's Knowledge Advisors are certified, highly experienced HR generalists who provide information resources and practical advice in response to SHRM members' HR-related questions. Knowledge Advisors develop HR-related content, including Q&As, for SHRM's website. This book is dedicated to the Knowledge Advisors.

Chapter 1
Affirmative Action Programs, the EEOC, and the Office of Federal Contract Compliance Programs

Q: What are the filing requirements for the EEO-I form?

The EEO-1 form is a report filed with the Equal Employment Opportunity Commission (EEOC), mandated by Title VII of the Civil Rights Act, as amended by the Equal Employment Opportunity Act. Title VII mandates that employers report on the racial/ethnic and gender composition of their workforce by specific job categories.

All employers that are located in the 50 states and the District of Columbia and that have at least 100 employees are required to file the EEO-1 survey annually with the EEOC. Federal government contractors and first-tier subcontractors with 50 or more employees and at least $50,000 in contracts must file as well. Reports must be filed by September 30 each year. Employment figures from any pay period in the third quarter (July through September) may be used. Although the EEOC has not defined how the 50 or 100 employees are to be counted, if an employer has met that threshold at some point during the year, and especially during the third quarter, it would be wise to either file or seek legal guidance to determine compliance.

The reporting system[1] and instructions[2] are available online.

If employers have filed an EEO-1 form in previous years, information on the form is pre-filled from the previous year.[3] First-time filers can find a simple registration form online at the EEOC website.[4] When registration is completed, the EEOC will issue a company number to the employer, and filers will be able to log into the system.

Q: How should employers report telecommuters and re-mote workers on the EEO-1 survey?

With the growing number of employers implementing flexible work arrangements, including telecommuting options, questions arise about reporting requirements such as those for the EEO-1 report.[5] Employers subject to Title VII of the Civil Rights Act with 100 or more employees and prime federal contractors with 50 or more employees are generally required to file the EEO-1 report by September 30 of each year. Companies will file either a single-establishment report (doing business in one physical location) or multi-establishment reports (doing business in two or more physical locations). The distinction between a single-establishment employer and a multi-establishment employer is critical as it will affect the number and type of equal employment opportunity (EEO) data reports that the employer will be required to submit. Multi-establishment employers are required to submit Headquarters and Establishment Reports as well as a Consolidated Report. Single-establishment employers must submit only one EEO-1 data report.

So how does an employer account for those employees who tele-commute or work out of their homes remotely? According to the EEO-1 report's "Frequently Asked Questions" section, employees who work from home, or telework, should be included on the report for the location to which they report. For example, the Headquarters Report must include those employees who work from home but report to the corporate office. Typically, any employees who telecommute will report in to a local, regional, or corporate office. For example, sales professionals, while working exclusively offsite, will generally report either to a regional sales office or a corporate sales department. Determining from which office the home-based employees are managed will be important to accurately report these individuals.

One additional complication that employers may encounter is the manner in which the employee's location information is recorded in the human resource information system (HRIS) or other internal reporting system. It is often necessary to record the employee's home address as his or her office address for tax purposes. Therefore, manual adjustments may need to be made to automated EEO-1 reports generated by the system to ensure that telecommuters are properly reported and do not appear on separate establishment reports.

Q: Should employers collect race and other demographic data during the application process or after employment starts?

Employers must consider obligations imposed by both the Equal Employment Opportunity Commission (EEOC) and the Office of Federal Contract Compliance Programs (OFCCP) to determine this answer.

In some instances, employers may be working to measure the validity of a selection procedure. For example, if an employer implements a test that measures typing skills, it may wish to determine if the test is eliminating protected class members at a higher rate than applicants who are not members of a protected class. It is necessary to collect information on an applicant's status as a protected class member to measure this. Both the EEOC and the OFCCP permit collecting this information in this case.

In other situations, the employer may be collecting data to satisfy EEO-1 reporting or affirmative action requirements. Employers subject to EEO-1 reporting,[6] but not to affirmative action requirements, would collect data on race and sex after employment commences. The EEO-1 report requires employers to provide information on their employees, but not on applicants.

Employers that are subject to affirmative action requirements are required to collect anonymous data on race and sex from applicants.[7] Some employers may also be voluntarily undertaking affirmative action efforts. In both cases, data can be collected before hire.

Q: What is an affirmative action program?

According to the U.S. Department of Labor's (DOL) Office of Federal Contract Compliance Programs (OFCCP):

> An affirmative action program is a management tool designed to ensure equal employment opportunity. A central premise underlying affirmative action is that, absent discrimination, over time a contractor's workforce, generally, will reflect the gender, racial and ethnic profile of the labor pools from which the contractor recruits and selects. Affirmative action programs contain a diagnostic component which includes a number of quantitative analyses designed to evaluate the composition of the workforce of the contractor and compare it to the composition of the relevant labor pools. Affirmative action programs also include action-oriented programs. If women and minorities are not being employed at a rate to be expected given their availability in the relevant labor pool, the contractor's affirmative action program includes specific practical steps designed to address this underutilization. Effective affirmative action programs also include internal auditing and reporting systems as a means of measuring the contractor's progress toward achieving the workforce that would be expected in the absence of discrimination.[8]

Q: When would a company need to have an affirmative action program?

Some employers assume that they must have an affirmative action program in place to comply with the requirements of Title VII of the Civil Rights Act and state equal employment opportunity (EEO) laws. In reality, though EEO laws prohibit unlawful discrimination against applicants and employees because of their race, gender, age, disability, or national origin, they usually do not require formal affirmative action programs. Employers generally implement formal affirmative action programs as a condition of doing business with the federal government, but an affirmative action program could also be required by a court as a remedy for discrimination or as a voluntary remedy for past patterns of discrimination.

Three separate laws require certain employers that do business with the federal government to implement affirmative action programs. Section 503 of the Rehabilitation Act requires contractors with contracts over $10,000 to take affirmative action with regard to qualified individuals with disabilities. The Vietnam Era Veterans' Readjustment Assistance Act (VEVRAA), as amended by the Jobs for Veterans Act, requires contractors to take affirmative action to employ and advance in employment veterans with service-connected disabilities, recently separated veterans, and other protected veterans. VEVRAA requires that employers with federal contracts entered before December 1, 2003, that also have 50 or more employees and contracts of $25,000 or more would be required to take affirmative action. Those with 50 or more employees and $50,000 in federal contracts would be required to have a written affirmative action program. For contracts entered on or after December 1, 2003, contractors with 50 or more employees and a federal contract of $100,000 or more would need a written affirmative action program.

Under Executive Order 11246,[9] federal contractors and subcontractors with 50 or more employees that have entered into at least one contract of $50,000 or more with the federal government must prepare and maintain a written program, which must be developed within 120 days from the commencement of the contract and must be updated annually. The program should cover recruitment, hiring, and promotion of women and minorities. Any depository of government funds in any amount or any financial institution that is an issuing and paying agent for U.S. savings bonds and savings notes in any amount must develop and maintain written affirmative action programs as well.

Affirmative action programs are not filed with the Office of Federal Contract Compliance Programs (OFCCP); they are kept by the contractor and must be produced in case of an audit by the OFCCP.

Many states also have affirmative action program requirements for state government contractors.

Courts may require employers to adopt affirmative action programs as a remedy for discrimination under Title VII. A court-ordered program generally:

- May not be overly burdensome on third parties (for example by requiring discharge or layoffs to achieve a racial balance).
- May not require the hiring or promotion of unqualified individuals.
- Must be temporary, lasting only until the program's goals are achieved.

Some employers adopt voluntary affirmative action programs to remedy past adverse impact against protected classes. For example, an employer may implement a program to encourage more women to apply for a job category traditionally dominated by men. However, any voluntary program must be narrowly tailored in time and scope so that it remedies only past discrimination.

Affirmative action programs are complex to create. Most employers do not choose to implement such programs unless they are required to do so.

Q: Where do employers get demographic data for affirmative action programs?

According to the U.S. Department of Labor's (DOL) Office of Federal Contract Compliance Programs (OFCCP):

> For calculating "external" availability, you want to consider who is qualified for the job within "the reasonable recruitment area" for that job. The "reasonable recruitment area" represents the area from which a contractor usually seeks or reasonably could seek workers for a particular job group. The reasonable recruitment area availability may be determined using the . . . Census Data Tool[10] on the Census Bureau web site.
>
> Please note that the regulation 41 CFR 60-2.14(d) requires contractors to use the most current and discrete statistical data available in determining availability estimates.[11] Census data is one example of an appropriate source of statistical information. Other sources include data from local job service offices and data from colleges or other training institutions.[12]

Q: Does the Office of Federal Contract Compliance Programs' rule on the definition of Internet applicant mean all electronic submissions of interest are applicants?

Certain criteria in addition to electronic submission must be met, according to the Office of Federal Contract Compliance Programs (OFCCP) in its final rule.

The OFCCP's final rule affects covered federal government contractors. The objective of OFCCP's rule was to create flexibility for contractors to come up with a system to ease record-keeping burdens and to assist in evaluating whether federal contractors are recruiting a diverse pool of qualified applicants and hiring new employees on a nondiscriminatory basis.

A candidate meets the definition of an Internet applicant if the following criteria are met:

- The individual submits an expression of interest in employment through the Internet or related electronic data technologies.
- The contractor considers the individual for a particular position.
- The individual's expression of interest indicates the individual possesses the basic objective qualifications for the position.
- The individual at no point in the contractor's selection process, prior to receiving an offer of employment, removes himself or herself from consideration or otherwise indicates that he or she is no longer interested in the position.

If the above criteria have been met, the contractor must retain all application or resume responses through the Internet or related electronic data technologies for two years. To minimize the potential volume of records, the OFCCP does not require contractors to retain records of individuals never considered for a position.

And under OFCCP's final rule, contractors may ignore responses to job posts that are not submitted in accordance with the contractor's standard procedures. Critically important for contactors to remember is that if the contractor considers expressions of interest through both the Internet and traditional means, the Internet applicant regulations apply to both types of submissions.

If the contractor prohibits electronic submissions for a position, the Internet definition of an applicant does not apply.

Q: When federal contractors subject to affirmative action requirements search online resume databases, are the individuals who submitted the resumes considered ap-

plicants under the Office of Federal Contract Compliance Programs' rules?

At least some of these individuals would likely be considered applicants, depending on the method the contractors used to search the online resume databases. If a contractor finds applicants among some of the resumes, it would need to retain the records for one year, if the contractor has fewer than 150 employees or does not have a contract of at least $150,000. Contractors with at least 150 employees or a contract of at least $150,000 are required to maintain the records for two years. That time period is measured from the time the record was created or from the time of the personnel action associated with that record, whichever is later.

When a contractor searches an external database, it is required to maintain copies of resumes of only those job seekers who meet the basic qualifications for the position and who are considered by the contractor. However, the key is the use of the word "consider." Recruiters often cast a broad net to fill vacancies quickly, but those who search too broadly on job boards risk weighing down their organizations with burdensome record-keeping requirements.

According to the Office of Federal Contract Compliance Programs (OFCCP), the definition of "considers the individual for employment in a particular position" means that the contractor "assesses the substantive information provided in the expression of interest with respect to any qualifications involved with a particular position."[13]

If there are a large number of expressions of interest, the contractor does not "consider the individual for employment in a particular position" if it uses data management techniques such as numeric limits or random generation to reduce the expressions of interest, as these techniques do not depend on any assessment of qualifications.

Some experts recommend that employers use a numeric limit

when searching external resume databases for positions that are likely to generate a large number of resumes, such as administrative assistants. However, if the contractor is searching for a position that would not result in a large number of resumes, such as an aerospace engineer, a numeric limit would probably not be necessary. A better search method might be for contractors to establish a search protocol under which they initially search the database for resumes indicating an interest in the position (for example, type of position, location, or salary sought by the job seeker). The OFCCP does not view use of information contained in a resume to gauge a job seeker's interest in a particular position to be "consideration" of a resume on the condition that the contractor is consistent in using the same procedure for all applicants. Using this method, the contractor would "consider" the subset of job seekers indicating an interest in the position to identify those meeting the basic qualifications. Under the Internet applicant rule the contractor would need to retain only those resumes considered that meet the basic qualifications for the position.

For example, assume a contractor is looking for someone with a bachelor's degree in engineering to work as an engineer in Cleveland, Ohio, for $60,000 per year. The contractor would like to search oodlesofresumes.com for candidates. A search of the resume database would produce 5,000 resumes of job seekers with a B.S. in engineering, 200 job seekers interested in working as an engineer in Cleveland for $60,000 a year, and 100 job seekers who both possess a B.S. in engineering and want to work as an engineer in Cleveland for $60,000 per year.

If the contractor's initial search is for anyone meeting the basic qualification of a B.S. in engineering, the search will produce 5,000 resumes, all of which would need to be retained. On the other hand, if the contractor initially searches the database for job seekers interested in working as an engineer in Cleveland for

$60,000, the search will produce 200 resumes. If the contractor searches the pool of 200 resumes for the basic qualification of a B.S. in engineering, the search will produce 100 resumes that must be retained.

If the contractor does not open the resume as a result of appropriate data management techniques that limit the number of resume "hits" that are reviewed, then the contractor has not "considered" that individual.

Chapter 2
Applicants

Q: Should employment applications request an applicant's Social Security number?

Though not unlawful to do so, given identity theft and general privacy concerns, employers generally should not request an applicant's Social Security number (SSN) on an employment application form, as an employment application is often viewed by individuals who do not have a need to know this information. An employment application should request only information directly related to an applicant's ability to perform a specific job. As a general practice, employers should request SSN information only when absolutely necessary, for example, in conjunction with a background check, when completing a W-4, or when enrolling the employee in benefits plans. This information should be requested separately from the employment application, and safeguards should be in place to protect and keep this information confidential. Employers should also implement procedures for safe disposal of this information once an employment decision has been made. Some states require security measures to be in place if applications asking for SSN information are transmitted over the Internet or are sent by mail in an unsealed envelope.

Q: Should certain questions not appear on an employment application?

An employment application should not include any questions that will produce a response that would indicate an applicant's protected class such as age, race, national origin, or disability.

Although many state and federal equal opportunity laws do not directly prohibit employers from asking such questions on an application, such inquiries may be used as evidence of an employer's intent to discriminate, unless the questions asked can be justified by some business purpose of the employer.

Information needed to conduct background checks should be obtained on a separate form authorizing the employer to conduct the check.

Some common inquiries to avoid are the following:

- Birth dates. Making inquiries about an applicant's birth date can give the perception that the employer is using age as a decision-making factor in the hiring process. If federal law or the employer's state law requires a minimum age for employment for certain occupations, then the employer can ask applicants if they are at least the required minimum age for employment.

- Graduation dates. Making inquiries of an applicant's school graduation date can reveal an applicant's age. To obtain information on whether an applicant holds a degree or a diploma, the employer can simply ask if the applicant has graduated and what degree was obtained.

- Military discharge information. Questions that are relevant to work experience and training received are permissible. However, an employer should not ask an applicant the reason he or she was discharged from the military or request to see military discharge papers (DD-214),[1] except when directly related to the job or to determine veterans' preference. Military discharge questions could result in obtaining medical disability information on an applicant, which is protected by the Americans with Disabilities Act (ADA). They could also lead to disparate impact based on race or violation of state military discharge anti-discrimination laws. To obtain information about an applicant's military service, an employer may make inquiries on the dates of military service, duties performed, rank during service at the time of discharge, pay during service and at the time of discharge, training received, and work experience.

- Previous sick days used in employment. In general, employers should avoid asking any questions about the amount of the sick leave taken in the applicant's past positions. The ADA prohibits discrimination and retaliation against applicants who have exercised their rights under this act.
- Race inquiries. An applicant's race or color should not be asked on an employment application. Some employers may track their applicants' race for affirmative action plans or compliance with the Uniform Guidelines on Employee Selection Procedures,[2] but tracking should be done apart from an application. Employers normally use a separate form or a tear-off section removed from the application; this information is not used in the selection process and is voluntary for the applicant.
- Citizenship. Inquiries about an individual's citizenship or country of birth are prohibited and can be perceived as discrimination on the basis of the individual's national origin. Applicants cannot be discriminated against based on their citizenship status, except in rare circumstances when required by federal contract. An employer can inquire if an applicant is legally eligible to work in the United States and inform the applicant that proof of his or her eligibility to work in the United States must be provided if selected for hire.
- Maiden name, "Miss," "Mrs.," and "Ms." Many states prohibit marital status discrimination, making any questions related to that status possible evidence of discriminatory hiring practices.

- Social Security number. Although asking applicants for their Social Security numbers (SSN) is not unlawful, requesting this information from applicants is not recommended due to identity theft and privacy concerns. Employers do not need this information until it is time to run a background check or to complete a W-4; therefore, including it on an application carries unnecessary risk. In addition, some states require security measures to be in place if applications asking for SSNs are transmitted electronically or mailed in an unsealed envelope.

Q: What are the pros and cons of accepting applications or resumes when an employer has no positions open?

Although accepting unsolicited applications or resumes may benefit some employers, the general practice has issues centered on how the employer defines "applicant."

Having an open-ended supply of applications on file can benefit some employers that have high turnover and many entry-level jobs, such as fast-food restaurants, because candidates can be contacted and positions filled quickly without the time and expense of advertising. Even employers with highly skilled positions, especially in niche industries or positions, could hire a valuable employee this way. Issues of record retention, unlawful discrimination, and possible affirmative action obligations, however, need to be weighed against this benefit to determine if the practice is right for the employer.

The first issue to consider is record retention. Both state and federal employment laws require employers to retain employment applications or resumes for at least one year, and possibly longer. The Office of Federal Contract Compliance (OFCCP) has narrowly defined who is an "Internet applicant" for federal contractors, but most employers are left to define "applicant" for themselves, through policy and practice.[3] Therefore, when an employer reviews unsolicited applications, those applications are seen as having been considered for employment, thereby becoming legal documents that must be retained. If an employer receives many unsolicited applications, the retention of these documents could be time-consuming and costly if storage requirements increase. Penalties could apply if they are not retained.

Secondly, reviewing unsolicited applications, when applied inconsistently, may expose the employer to claims of unlawful discrimination. Federal and state employment nondiscrimination laws require that covered employers conduct their recruitment and hiring in an entirely nondiscriminatory way with respect to the various protected classes, such as age, gender, and disability.[4] These laws prohibit not only intentional discrimination but also unintentional discrimination, that is, using neutral selection criteria that have the effect of disproportionately excluding people based on their protected status without sufficient justification. Having an inconsistently followed policy or practice of accepting or not accepting unsolicited resumes could make it appear that the employer is discriminating against protected classes. For instance, if applicant A's unsolicited resume is accepted and leads to a job, but applicant B's resume is not accepted, applicant B may be able to make a case for unlawful discrimination based on protected class.

Finally, federal contractors with affirmative action obligations must capture applicant demographic data;[5] without a clear practice and policy in place, this data will be missed, and OFCCP violations could apply.

If an employer decides to accept unsolicited resumes or applications, it should accept all unsolicited resumes or applications, and it should have a consistently followed written policy for handling them. The policy should have clear guidelines on how the documents will be reviewed and by whom, how long they will be retained, and how the applicant will be notified if he or she is or is not considered for future open positions. If an employer does not accept unsolicited resumes, the organization's website should state that unsolicited resumes or applications are not accepted. Also, front desk personnel should be made aware of this policy and be provided with a script to use when individuals ask for an application or wish to drop off a resume.

Q: Do federal or state laws prohibit employers from asking applicants about arrests and convictions?

No federal law clearly prohibits an employer from asking about arrest and conviction records, but using such records as an absolute measure to prevent an individual from being hired could limit the employment opportunities of some protected groups. In April 2012, the Equal Employment Opportunity Commission (EEOC) provided guidance on employer use of arrest and conviction records that seeks to clarify its longstanding position on the limited use of these records in employment.[6]

Given that an arrest alone does not necessarily mean that an individual has committed a crime, the employer should not assume that the applicant committed the offense. Instead, the employer should allow the applicant the opportunity to explain the circumstances of the arrest(s) and make a reasonable effort to determine whether the explanation is reliable.

Even if the employer believes that the applicant did engage in the conduct for which he or she was arrested, this information should prevent the applicant from employment only to the extent that it is evident that the applicant cannot be trusted to perform the duties of the position when considering the following factors:

- The nature of the job.
- The nature and seriousness of the offense for which the applicant was arrested.
- The length of time since the arrest occurred.

This guidance is also true for a conviction.

Several state laws limit the use of arrest and conviction records by prospective employers. These range from laws and rules prohibiting the employer from asking the applicant any questions about arrest records to those restricting the employer's use of conviction data in making an employment decision.

In some states, although there is no restriction placed on the employer, there are protections provided to the applicants with regard to what information they are required to report.

The Fair Credit Reporting Act (FCRA) imposes a number of requirements on employers that wish to investigate applicants for employment through the use of a consumer credit report or a criminal records check. This law requires the employer to advise the applicant in writing that a background check will be conducted, to obtain the applicant's written authorization to acquire the records, and to notify the applicant that a poor credit history or conviction will not automatically result in disqualification from employment.

Certain other disclosures are required at the employee's request and prior to taking any adverse action based on the reports obtained.

Q: Can a company have a policy to disqualify applicants who fail drug tests from the possibility of future employment?

Such a policy would violate the Americans with Disabilities Act (ADA) for employers subject to that act. According to Technical Guidance from the Equal Employment Opportunity Commission (EEOC),

> Persons addicted to drugs, but who are no longer using drugs illegally and are receiving treatment for drug addiction or who have been rehabilitated successfully, are protected by the ADA from discrimination on the basis of past drug addiction.[7]

See also Questions 15 and 16 in the EEOC's document *How to Comply with the Americans with Disabilities Act: A Guide for Restaurants and Other Food Service Employers.*[8] Employers should understand that it is not a violation of the ADA for an employer to require tests for the illegal use of drugs. An employer has the right to discharge or deny employment to persons who currently engage in the illegal use of drugs. However, employers may violate the ADA in denying future employment based on past failure of a drug test. *The EEOC's Technical Assistance Manual* is quite clear on this point:

> For example: An addict who is currently in a drug rehabilitation program and has not used drugs illegally for some time is not excluded from the protection of the ADA. This person will be protected by the ADA because s/he has a history of addiction, or if s/he is "regarded as" being addicted. Similarly, an addict who is rehabilitated or who has successfully completed a supervised rehabilitation program and is no longer illegally using drugs is not excluded from the ADA.[9]

Accordingly, an employer subject to the ADA should not have a policy stating that employees who fail a drug test will be ineligible for rehire, nor should an employer apply such a restriction even absent a formal policy.

Conversely, if an individual tests positive on a test for the illegal use of drugs, the individual will be considered a current drug user under the ADA when the test correctly indicates that the individual is engaging in the illegal use of a controlled substance. "Current" drug use means that the illegal use of drugs occurred recently enough to justify an employer's reasonable belief that involvement with drugs is an ongoing problem.

The EEOC provides the following example:

> An applicant or employee who tests positive for an illegal drug cannot immediately enter a drug rehabilitation program and seek to avoid the possibility of discipline or termination by claiming that s/he now is in rehabilitation and is no longer using drugs illegally. A person who tests positive for illegal use of drugs is not entitled to the protection that may be available to former users who have been or are in rehabilitation.[10]

To ensure that drug use is not recurring, an employer may request evidence that an individual is participating in a drug rehabilitation program or may request the results of a drug test.

As with other disabilities, an individual who claims that he or she was discriminated against because of past or perceived illegal drug addiction may be asked to prove that he or she has a record of, or is regarded as having, an addiction to drugs.

Note, the answer would be the same for alcoholism as for illegal drug addiction.

Q: May an employer ask to see an applicant's prior performance reviews?

Though asking to view an applicant's prior performance reviews is generally permissible, the real issue is whether it is an effective HR practice.

Some employers believe the rationale for requesting performance review information during the hiring process is to determine in advance the type of employee the applicant will become. However, employers do not have an effective way to determine if there is a direct correlation or if a performance review is a reliable or valid predicator of future performance.

Performance reviews, evaluations, or appraisals at best are a summary of past employee performance at a specific point in time. Most performance review processes are subject to various forms of controversy, and numerous articles have been written about the problems with rater bias and subjectivity.

The issue is further compounded when one looks at the transferability of performance review information from one employer to another. How effectively and meaningfully can one employer glean and use the information from performance appraisals from another organization, particularly when the potential employer is unaware of or unfamiliar with the rating scales, values, and culture of other organizations? For example, one organization may value innovation whereas another organization may value strict adherence to established rules. The applicant may be applying for a position with an organization specifically because of this cultural-fit issue with his or her current or former employer. If the hiring company used performance review information from the current or former employer to weed out the applicant, it could miss an opportunity to hire a stellar performer for its organization.

Employers should also consider the effect of other related issues, including concerns about discrimination if the practice is not consistently applied, particularly without a job-related purpose, as well as concerns about the applicant's privacy. If employers decide to go forward with this practice, they should develop guidelines about how best to obtain and use the information, and the consequences to applicants if they fail to provide the information.

A more effective practice might be to obtain the applicant's written permission to confer with current or former supervisors once a conditional offer of employment is made. Supervisory referrals may provide more useful information that can be helpful in determining not only whether to hire the employee but the types of supervision the applicant best responds to. This is an accepted practice and less likely to be met with resistance from applicants or their supervisors.

Q: What accommodations should a company make for applicants with disabilities?

The Americans with Disabilities Act (ADA), as amended, requires employers to provide reasonable accommodations to employees or job applicants who are qualified individuals with disabilities, unless doing so would cause undue hardship. An accommodation is any change in the work environment or the way things are usually done that will enable an individual with a disability to enjoy equal employment opportunities. Accommodations are also required during the job application process, if needed.

An employer is obligated to provide accommodations for known disabilities. Generally, it is the responsibility of the individual with the disability to inform the employer of the need for accommodation. This need can be stated in "plain English," and the individual is not required to mention the ADA, to fill out forms, or to use the term "reasonable accommodation."[11] The employer must inform employees and applicants of its obligation under the ADA to provide reasonable accommodations. Notices should be posted in conspicuous places where employees and applicants can see them. Notices can be included in job applications, job vacancy notices, or internal postings or can be communicated orally.

The Equal Employment Opportunity Commission (EEOC) issued specific guidelines on reasonable accommodation and job applicants. When the applicant has not asked for an accommodation, the employer may tell applicants what the hiring process involves (for example, an interview, timed written test, or job demonstration) and may ask applicants whether they will need a reasonable accommodation for this process.

The EEOC guidelines clearly state that individuals with disabilities who meet initial requirements to be considered for a job should not be excluded from the application process because the employer speculates (a speculation based on the request for reasonable accommodation to complete the application process) that the individual will be unable to perform the job. The need for reasonable accommodation for the application process should be evaluated separately from any accommodations needed to perform the job.

Q: Is it illegal to ask for an applicant's or employee's date of birth?

No law prohibits an employer from asking for date of birth (DOB). How the employer uses that information is important. The Age Discrimination in Employment Act (ADEA) protects workers by prohibiting discrimination against workers age 40 and over in any employment or employment-related decision. Therefore, the employer should take care not to use or appear to be using the DOB in making employment or employment-related decisions.

Employers' background check vendors will probably confirm that the DOB is required to facilitate the most effective background check. Companies should consider these ideas for reducing their exposure in requesting the DOB for the purpose of running background checks:

- The background check authorization form and request for DOB should be separate from the employment application, and the response to that DOB request should never be forwarded with the application or resume to the hiring managers or anyone else who does not need to know the applicant's DOB.
- The employer should limit its request for the DOB to the background check authorization form. The employer may consider using the vendor's background check authorization form with the vendor's logo and company name rather than

having the employer's name or logo on the form.

- The employer could ask the vendor if an equally effective background check could be performed by having just the month and day of birth.
- The applicant's DOB should be shared on a strict need-to-know basis only (that is, the background check vendor or employer representative conducting the background check).
- The employer could ask the vendor if it can provide the service of collecting the DOB for the employer, such as through a toll-free telephone or fax number.
- The employer could provide the applicant with a stamped envelope addressed to the background check vendor for the applicant to return the authorization form.

In addition, the employer may like to include a statement similar to the following with its request for the DOB:

> Applicants are considered, and employees are treated during employment, without regard to age, race, color, religion, sex, national origin, marital or veteran status, medical condition, or disability. Date of birth is required from all applicants and employees to facilitate a background check.

Q: How can employers protect themselves from liability when giving references?

Employers may be liable if they provide a negative reference for unlawfully discriminatory reasons, in retaliation for a former employee's complaining of an illegal activity, or if they give a defamatory reference or disclose confidential facts that constitute an invasion of privacy.

Defamation occurs when one person makes false written or oral statements that harm another person's reputation. Defamation takes two forms: libel and slander. Libel occurs when the defamatory statements are written, slander when the defamatory statements are spoken. For a former employee to prove a defamation case, that employee must prove that false statements were made. The worker must also prove that the false statements were communicated to a third party, usually to a prospective employer or to a background-checking agency. Finally, the person must prove that injury occurred as a result of the false statement. Injury in employment reference cases usually takes the form of the former employee's being refused future employment based on the allegedly defamatory statements.

To protect the company from defamation suits, the most conservative approach is to give no references at all. But this tactic can backfire in the form of negligent referral lawsuits that can be brought by the former employee's future employer if the company withheld important negative information about that former employee. It also prevents the company from helping a valued former employee to advance in his or her career.

Many states have recognized the reluctance of many employers to disclose this type of information on former employees and have passed legislation known as "job reference immunity" laws. These immunity laws will not protect an employer that knowingly gives false or misleading information, but they will protect employers that provide truthful, good-faith references to other employers.

Another approach is to provide limited references. In giving even limited references, the truth is the best defense against defamation allegations. Ways to limit any possible liability in disclosing reference information include the following:

- Providing only information that can be documented, such as dates of employment and title.
- Requiring the former employee to sign releases indicating what information the company is allowed to disclose.

- Training managers and supervisors on how to provide references.
- Requiring all managers and supervisors to refer requests for references to the HR department.
- Developing a policy and communicating it to managers and supervisors.

Q: How should a U.S. employer evaluate a foreign degree?

The U.S. Department of Education (DOE) does not evaluate foreign degrees, but employers may use credential evaluation services to determine if a foreign degree meets their job requirements. These privately owned services are available for a price and are not regulated by state or federal government.

DOE advises individuals seeking to work in the U.S. to contact the HR office of their prospective employer or a state licensing board for specific professions for instructions on how to have their education evaluated.

Employers may ask applicants to use a specific credential evaluation service to analyze foreign qualifications and recommend how they should be compared to similar U.S. qualifications, including educational degrees and professional credentials. Costs vary depending on how complex the evaluations are and how difficult it is to access the information. The applicant often pays for the service, but employers may also pay for it.

For certain regulated occupations that require specific degrees, licenses, or other qualifications, a state licensing board may recommend a particular credential evaluation service to use. More than 50 professional occupations are licensed in all U.S. states and territories, and most require post-secondary education or training.

Though not an exhaustive list, the DOE document, "Recognition of Foreign Qualifications: Professional Recognition," lists professions that have recognized U.S. accrediting agencies for pre-professional education.[12]

If no specific credentialing services are recommended, an employer may choose any service. An employer may also consult with two national associations, which have set standards for the industry: the National Association of Credential Evaluation Services and the Association of International Credential Evaluators, Inc.

Applicants from other countries who hold qualifications that are based on noneducational routes to licensure (such as noncredit training) may have difficulty obtaining full recognition of the qualifications. They may be able to receive partial or full undergraduate credit for their work experience or noneducational licenses, but they must come to the U.S. first. Two national associations provide these types of recognitions: the National College Credit Recommendation Service and the College Level Examination Program.

Q: Must all employers check applicants against a terrorist list before hiring?

Under the U.S. Treasury Department, the Office of Foreign Assets Control (OFAC) administers and enforces economic sanctions against certain countries and certain individuals, such as drug traffickers and terrorists. To help enforce these sanctions, the OFAC publishes a frequently updated document called the "Specially Designated Nationals List," or the SDN List, which identifies individuals, companies, and other entities that U.S. persons are prohibited from dealing with.[13] Compliance with these sanctions means all U.S. persons (which, by definition, includes employers) cannot engage in any dealings with these countries or individuals, including hiring individuals on the list. Therefore, although checking the list is not specifically required, hiring someone on the list is prohibited. Under the guidance of legal counsel, employers must address the following concerns.

First, the list is open to the public on the department's website, but it is not easy to sort through. Individual and organization names are mixed together, and there are often many aliases. Dates of birth are often missing, or several alternatives are listed, and addresses are not specific and may only list country and city. The list also contains many common Latino and Arabic names. All these factors hinder making a positive identification, and employers may unfairly deny employment to an innocent individual. Federal and state discrimination and other civil liberties claims could follow if these hiring practices are not conducted carefully and with expert guidance.

Second, when an employer does find a match on the list, it would then be required to notify the OFAC. Although the OFAC offers some guidance on when a match should be reported (on its website, under "Resource Center," "FAQs," and "Sanctions[14]"), time and effort may be required to make this determination, report it, and follow up with the OFAC before making a final hiring decision. With the OFAC itself reporting that the chances of a match are not great, employers will need to determine if consulting the SDN—and at what point—in the hiring process would be in their best interests.

Many background checking companies offer an add-on service to check not only the SDN but various other lists, such as those compiled by the United Nations, Interpol, and the Federal Bureau of Investigations (FBI). Employers should know what lists will be checked and how best to use that information in their hiring practices.

Q: What are the federal record retention guidelines for applications and resumes of candidates who are not selected?

Several federal laws apply to the retention of applications and resumes. Organizations must comply with all applicable laws, and, therefore, retention should be based on the longest length required under any or all laws.

Major federal anti-discrimination laws addressing the retention of employment records and, specifically, hiring records, include Title VII of the Civil Rights Act, the Americans with Disabilities Act (ADA), and the Age Discrimination in Employment Act (ADEA).

Title VII and the ADA apply to employers of 15 or more employees. The ADEA applies to employers with 20 or more employees. Employers covered under these laws must retain hiring records for each position for at least one year from the date of the hiring decision (that is, the date the position was filled). Hiring records include all applications and resumes considered for the position, selection testing (for example, employment tests and drug tests), and investigations (reference checks and background or credit checks).

In addition, under the anti-discrimination laws, if there is a pending charge or claim of discrimination against the organization, all relevant hiring records must be retained until the conclusion of the case.

Federal contractors and subcontractors may be subject to longer record retention requirements. In accordance with Executive Order 11246,[15] federal contractors or subcontractors with 150 or more employees and at least $150,000 in federal contracts or subcontracts must retain their hiring records (including applications and resumes for all candidates) for two years from when the hiring decision was made. Any federal contractors or subcontractors with fewer than 150 employees or less than $150,000 in contracts must retain hiring records for only one year.

Chapter 3

Background Investigations

Q: When must employers comply with the Fair Credit Reporting Act?

The Fair Credit Reporting Act (FCRA) governs how employers obtain and handle consumer reports, affecting employers that gather reports on their applicants and employees prior to making business decisions.

The FCRA requires employers to disclose that consumer reports may be used for employment decisions and to secure consent from employees or applicants to obtain these reports. If consumer reports provide information that results in an adverse employment action against an individual, the employer must provide the person with a copy of the report and his or her FCRA rights.

Many employers are uncertain which reports are covered by the law. According to the Federal Trade Commission (FTC), an FCRA consumer report is any written, oral, or other communication of any information by a consumer reporting agency bearing on a consumer's credit worthiness, credit standing, credit capacity, character, general reputation, personal characteristics, or mode of living. In the employment context, this definition may, for example, include credit reports, criminal history reports, driving records, and other background check reports created by a third party, such as drug tests.

The Fair and Accurate Credit Transactions (FACT) Act, which amended the FCRA, still requires employers to notify employees of investigations, but only after investigations have concluded.

The FTC then issued the FACT Act disposal rule, detailing how employers should dispose of consumer reports to reduce the possibility of identity theft.[1] In essence, employers should shred (or burn) their consumer reports, not just throw them in the trash.

FCRA reports exclude pre-placement or fitness-for-duty physicals, or any reports generated internally such as internal reference checking. Drug tests will likely be covered if reported to the employer from a credit reporting agency.[2] Due to the complexity of the FCRA, prior to outsourcing any investigative check of applicants or employees, employers should ensure that they are compliant with the law.

Q: Why should an employer verify an applicant's education?

Unfortunately, not all applicants are honest on their resumes and employment applications, and this deception may include embellishing or outright lying about education. Studies continue to show an increase in the number of discrepancies between what is shown on education records and the information provided by the applicant. There have also been recent news stories of fraud—from a well-known electronic retailer's CEO to a cable network television personality—illustrating that falsification of education and credentials is a problem employers need to take seriously.

In addition to lying about education, some employees obtain documentation from diploma mills that may appear to be valid. Diploma mills are illegitimate colleges or universities that provide degrees for a fee with little or no coursework required. The services of diploma mills can be quite extensive, including not only very legitimate-appearing diplomas but also verification services as well as transcripts and letters of recommendation.

Diploma mills affect the employment credibility of individuals and can also affect an employer's tuition reimbursement program. In 2002, the Government Accountability Office (then called the General Accounting Office) reported results of a three-year investigation, which included significant proof that government funds were being spent on bogus degrees by overcompensating employees and reimbursing for tuition that was illegitimate.

Recruiters and employers are encouraged to verify credentials directly through the educational institution or by using a background screening service. Many colleges and universities have a degree verification program or refer employers to the National Student Clearinghouse, to which employers pay a nominal fee for the verification.[3] Another option is to ask the employee to have a certified college transcript sent directly to the employer from the school. However, using transcripts or contacting the school directly will not necessarily weed out false information from a diploma mill, for example, if the school is fictitious. If employers question the authenticity of the information provided, they should refer to the U.S. Department of Education's accreditation database[4] or to the Council for Higher Education Accreditation[5] to determine if the educational institution is legitimate.

Q: Are there any restrictions when performing background checks or drug tests on minors?

There are a number of factors to consider when conducting background checks or drug tests on minors seeking employment.

The U.S. Department of Justice has reported that on a national level crimes among juveniles have continued to decrease significantly since 1980. Despite this decrease, and depending on job requirements and company policies, employers may still have justifiable security and safety concerns with seasonal, temporary, or other labor needs met by minors. Running third-party background checks on minors falls under the Fair Credit Reporting Act (FCRA), just as they would for any other applicant or employee; therefore, careful understanding of the nature of a minor's consent is necessary for employers to be protected.

Before seeking consent in conjunction with pre-employment screenings, employers should understand that minors are generally not able to legally provide consent, as persons under the age of 18 (lower in some states) are unable to enter legally binding agreements, with few exceptions. Minors are not expected to have the maturity necessary to fully understand the terms and obligations of a legal agreement or contract, so although they may sign a release for pre-employment screenings, it will not likely be binding, leaving the employer unprotected. Parents have the legal authority over minors; therefore, they can give their consent to the screenings, which will be legally binding. Employers wishing to run these screens on minors and be protected should require parental or legal guardian consent. When the minor is not able to provide parental consent, employers should consult with their attorney for a recommended practice.

Even when parental consent is obtained, however, not all records an employer usually requests in these screenings will be available on minors. For example, the majority of criminal records for minors are sealed, making them unattainable. An exception would be in limited situations where a minor was convicted as an adult. Additionally, minors generally are unable to obtain credit until age 18, making credit history unlikely to exist. Past employment and educational records, however, should be available, and personal references can also be obtained. Therefore, when using pre-employment screening information in hiring minors, employers may need to adjust their policies and practices in terms of what information they will have available to use. Employers may wish to seek legal counsel to draft a screening policy that best protects them when hiring minors.

Finally, as with adult applicants and employees, minors are afforded the same rights under Title VII of the Civil Rights Act, including the provision that all pre-employment and post-hire screenings should demonstrate job-relatedness and be part of a uniformly applied practice to those jobs demonstrating such requirements.

Q: What should an employer look for when selecting a background check vendor?

Most employers do some sort of background checking of applicants, and many choose to outsource this time-consuming and compliance-heavy activity. Though engaging the services of a vendor will not relieve the employer of any legal hiring obligations, selecting one that is reliable, trustworthy, and accurate will help meet those obligations.

Some things to consider when interviewing or sending a request for proposal to a vendor include the following:

- Accuracy and quality. What quality assurance and compliance practices are in place? How does the vendor stay abreast of current federal and state laws? What are its Fair Credit Reporting Act (FCRA)-related practices? How are new employees trained? Is the vendor a member of and accredited by the National Association of Professional Background Screeners (NAPBS)?[6]
- Speed. How quickly will results be sent to the employer? Expectations should be no longer than one week, shorter for limited checks and longer for more extensive checking services.
- Client retention rate and references. What is the retention rate of the vendor's clients? Will it provide at least three current client references?
- Sources of information. Where does the vendor obtain its information from? Data should be from direct sources,

such as courthouse records, former employers, and universities. Are these searches conducted by phone, by e-mail, or through online databases?

- Services offered. Does the vendor offer the services the employer needs, such as personal and professional references, criminal histories, educational inquiries, and driving records? Does it offer only domestic checks or also international ones, if needed? Are these checks bundled, or can the employer select different reports as needed?

- Technology, data security, and accessibility. What type of user interface does the vendor offer? Can data requests be submitted from more than one user? What are the reporting options? What data security features are in place to protect the employer and potential employees?

- Support services. What are the vendor's hours of operation? Can requests be submitted 24/7? Will the employer have a dedicated representative? How will escalations be handled? How is client satisfaction measured?

- Payment terms. What are the payment terms? Is there a minimum contract length, or pay as you go? Are discounts offered for bundled options?

When searching for a vendor, SHRM members might consider asking other members for their recommendations on SHRM's member bulletin board, HR Talk, or on SHRM's social media site, SHRM Connect. Employers might also review the list of accredited vendors on the NAPBS website.

Q: Which employees must be processed through E-Verify? Can employers verify all employees?

Once an employer becomes a covered contractor subject to an E-Verify clause in its federal contract, it must enroll in E-Verify within 30 days. Within 90 days of enrolling in E-Verify, contractors must start processing all new hires through E-Verify. All existing employees assigned to the federal contract must also be processed through E-Verify within 90 days of enrolling in the E-Verify system. According to the U.S. Citizenship and Immigration Services (USCIS) FAQs on federal contractors and E-Verify,

> The rule defines an "employee assigned to the federal contract" as any employee hired after November 6, 1986, who is directly performing work in the United States under a contract that includes the clause committing the contractor to use E-Verify. An employee is not considered to be directly performing work under the contract if the employee normally performs support work, such as indirect or overhead functions, and does not perform any substantial duties under the contract. Those who have an active federal agency HSPD-12 credential or who have been granted and hold an active U.S. Government security clearance do not need to be verified.[7]

Employers can choose to use E-Verify for all existing employees hired after November 6, 1986. This may be a preferred choice for employers that do not want to closely monitor and track which employees are assigned to federal contract work.

Q: When must an employer respond to a verification of employment request, and what information must or can be given?

Verification of employment (VOE) requests on current or former employees can come to an employer from government agencies, mortgage lenders, prospective employers, collection agents, and others. They usually seek to verify employment dates, wages, likelihood of continued employment or eligibility for rehire, and reason for termination. When must employers respond to such requests, and what information must or should they divulge?

Certainly, only truthful, supportable information should be shared, regardless to whom it is given. States have job reference immunity laws that can cover VOE requests, and if truthful information is given in good faith, the employer will likely be protected from defamation claims. Additionally, a signed consent from the employee should be obtained when possible, with some state immunity laws requiring consent to be protected.

Though not always clear-cut, requests from federal and state government agencies and offices often require compliance, whereas most other requests do not. A request from a government agency often cites a regulation requiring the information; if not, employers can generally feel confident about sharing the information asked for, as a good faith effort to comply. These requests are often to verify wages for court decisions (such as child support) or government programs, to uncover fraudulent use of government services, or even to help an employee prove his or her identity was stolen. These requests are usually specific in terms of the information needed, and again, any truthful information provided should not subject the employer to legal claims.

Employers are not required by law to complete VOEs from mortgage lenders, but few employers would choose to disadvantage their employees by ignoring the request. Employers may require written consent from employees before providing information to mortgage lenders and perhaps have a policy that employees must notify human resources of upcoming requests. In general, though, employers complete these with truthful responses regarding the current employment situation without guaranteeing continued employment or defaming the employee.

Prospective employers may ask any number of questions, from final wage information to job performance information. Each employer needs to determine if it will require a signed release for this information and what type of information it will share. Certain industries, such as health care, and positions, such as those working with children, may have additional state requirements to share information that may stop a negligent hire.

Employers generally do not need to respond to collections agencies and anyone else seeking information, and before sharing information with them, employers may wish to seek legal counsel on a recommended policy on handling these requests that will best protect the employer.

Chapter 4
Drug and Alcohol Testing

Q: Must all companies follow the Fair Credit Reporting Act guidelines for drug tests?

It depends on the situation. Employers often use the term "background check" to describe a process that can include one or any combination of screening tools, including criminal records checks, credit reports, motor vehicle reports, reference checks, and drug test results. The Fair Credit Reporting Act (FCRA) requires, among other things, that employers provide disclosure and obtain consent before securing a consumer report.

The Federal Trade Commission (FTC), which governs and enforces the FCRA, describes a consumer report as follows:

> "A consumer report contains information about your personal and credit characteristics, character, general reputation and lifestyle. To be covered by the FCRA, a report must be prepared by a CRA [consumer reporting agency]—a business that assembles such reports for other businesses."[1]

The FTC explains,

> An intermediary that retains copies of tests performed by drug labs and regularly sells this information to third parties for a fee is a CRA whose reports of drug test results are "consumer reports" covered by the FCRA.[2]

In summary, some background check companies include drug test results in their reporting services. In this case, these drug tests would likely be considered a consumer report. On the other hand, if an employer obtains the information directly from a drug-testing lab, it is less likely to be considered a consumer report and subject to the FCRA. The FTC offers specific guidance on drug tests as consumer reports.[3]

Q: What are the requirements for drug testing commercial vehicle operators and employees who drive as part of the job?

The Omnibus Transportation Employee Testing Act requires employers to set forth drug and alcohol testing requirements for employees who operate commercial vehicles. The intent of the act is to increase transportation safety by mandating such testing for individuals in safety-sensitive positions.

The U.S. Department of Transportation (DOT) publishes rules in accordance with the act for employers that must conduct the testing. Employers in the aviation, trucking, railroad, mass transit, pipeline, or maritime industries must implement required testing. DOT agencies, including the Federal Motor Carrier Safety Administration, the Federal Railroad Administration, the Federal Aviation Administration, the Federal Transit Administration, and the Pipeline and Hazardous Materials Safety Administration, as well as the U.S. Coast Guard, have industry-specific regulations for testing employees who perform safety-sensitive functions.

The act mandates pre-employment, reasonable suspicion, post-accident, random, and follow-up/return-to-duty drug and alcohol testing of employees in positions requiring a commercial driver's license and defined as safety-sensitive. The law prohibits commercial motor vehicle drivers from performing safety-sensitive functions after an alcohol test result indicating a 0.02 percent alcohol concentration or a positive drug test result. The law also prohibits drivers from using alcohol or illegal drugs while on duty.

Employees covered by the act should be tested under the following circumstances:

- When assigned to a position requiring a commercial driver's license.
- On a random basis.
- After an accident that resulted in the employee's being issued a citation for a moving vehicle violation or in a fatality.
- For reasonable cause based on observed behavior or appearance.
- Before being allowed to return to a covered position after having tested positive for drug or alcohol abuse.

Although DOT regulations mandate the types of testing and the procedures to adhere to following a positive test result, the regulations do not address employment decisions such as hiring, firing, or leaves of absence. These decisions are up to the employer, in accordance with other applicable laws such as the Americans with Disabilities Act.

Employers are required by law to provide certain records of former employees' DOT drug and alcohol testing history to their new employers, though only when the former employee signs a specific written release regarding that information. Employees or employers that violate the provisions of this law are subject to fines for each offense.

Chapter 5
Employment Offers

Q: Can an employer rescind a job offer?

Because an employer's rescindment of a job offer could have legal consequences, an attorney's advice should always be sought before rescinding the offer.

Even if an employer has stated on all offers that employment is at will and can be terminated at any time, there is the concept of the employer's making a "promise" of a job. If the promise of a job is rescinded, it could cause economic and emotional harm to the candidate. For example, the candidate could end up jobless because he or she has given notice at the current job, the candidate may have incurred relocation costs, or he or she may suffer emotional distress.

Promissory estoppel is a legal doctrine that supports a harmed party in enforcing such promises made, even if a true contract did not exist. Many candidates have successfully used this argument to win their cases in court, and some have used additional arguments connected to breach of the implied covenant of good faith and fair dealing; fraud and misrepresentation; and reckless, negligent, or intentional misinterpretation and infliction of emotional distress.

When an employment contract itself actually exists and was signed by the parties, breach of contract can be added to that list of claims, and an employer could easily find itself on the losing end of such a battle.

In all cases, regardless of whether the employer feels the candidate suffered losses, a complete legal review of the situation should be conducted. It should include interviews with all employees who spoke with the candidate and may have inadvertently made promises to that person. The offer should then be rescinded only with the approval of legal counsel.

Q: What factors should I consider when determining where to place a new hire within the pay range?

There are several factors, monetary and nonmonetary, to consider when determining the base pay for a new hire. The key is to create an offer that meets the business strategy and the individual's expectations, while complying with all applicable laws.

Business Strategy

The decision-maker should consider such business-related factors as the following:

- Organization's compensation philosophy. Do the company's industry, business objectives, and location demand the premium rate for this job?
- Departmental budget. Does the budget allow for any flexibility in the offer?
- Internal equity. What are other employees in this same job, in the same department, or at the same job level being paid?
- Market price or external influences. Is this job difficult to fill, or is it hard to find qualified candidates in this location or industry?
- Candidate's level of experience. How many years of relevant experience does this person have?
- Candidate's education and certification levels. Does this person have degrees or professional certifications that will benefit the employer?
- Geographic differential. Is the job located in an area that has a higher cost of living or that demands higher salaries?

Individual's Expectation

As to the individual's expectations, considerations should include the following:

- Base pay expectation. Is the person's base pay expectation in alignment with the offer, and if not, are other incentives sufficient?
- Variable or incentive compensation. What type of pay-for-performance system or additional compensation is given periodically?
- Benefits package. What is the level of coverage and the cost to an employee for medical, dental, vision, prescription drug, flexible spending accounts, 401(k) (match and vesting schedule), other retirement accounts, employee assistance program, disability, life, and accidental death and dismemberment insurance?
- Work/life balance. How much paid leave (for example, vacation and sick time) would accrue?
- Development opportunities. What is the tuition reimbursement policy? Does the company support professional certifications or attendance at professional conferences and seminars?
- Commute. How would the commute between home and work be affected? Are flexible work schedules and telecommuting options offered?
- Candidate's current total compensation package. What is the person's current base pay, variable pay, benefits package, work/life situation, career development opportunities, and commute?

Legally Defensible?

Any job offer must comply with all applicable federal and state laws, including the following:

- Title VII of the Civil Rights Act, which bars discrimination in employment on the basis of race, color, gender, religion, and national origin.

- The Pregnancy Discrimination Act, which amended Title VII to include pregnant women.
- The Equal Pay Act, which amended the Fair Labor Standards Act to prohibit employers from taking gender into account when compensating men and women performing work requiring equal skill, effort, and responsibility.
- The Lilly Ledbetter Fair Pay Act, which amended Title VII to clarify when unlawful employment acts were considered to be made in terms of pay.
- The Americans with Disabilities Act, as amended, which protects qualified individuals with disabilities.
- The Age Discrimination in Employment Act, which prohibits age-based discrimination against applicants and employees over 40.
- State nondiscrimination laws, which vary from state to state and may be broader than federal laws.

Q. When a company hires a new employee, must the new hire be provided with an offer letter? What should be included in an offer letter to avoid the perception of an employment contract?

Although not required, providing a candidate a written offer is a good practice. Following up a verbal offer with a written offer will not only set expectations for the new employee, but also clarify any matters that were discussed during the interview phase. For example, an offer letter can provide details about the start date, any contingencies, such as passing a drug test or background check, the job title, and basic salary and benefits information. An offer letter can be an important piece of documentation in the event the new hire wants to negotiate salary or benefits.

Signing an offer letter confirms that the candidate has accepted the position and its terms. However, employers should be mindful of the language used in the offer letter, or it may be construed as an employment contract or agreement.

In an effort to avoid creating a contractual agreement, the letter should contain a statement that the employment is at will. Employment at will is a doctrine that means no contract is in place between the employer and the employee, and neither is beholden to the other. When a contract is introduced, the employment-at-will relationship is negated. Eliminating verbiage about employment for a definite period of time or promises about future earnings or bonuses is a consistent way to mitigate risk in the event that an employee files suit based on language in the offer letter that implies an employment commitment between the employer and the employee.

Knowing the provisions typically included in an employment contract will help HR professionals avoid inadvertently adding these elements to their offer letters. Common topics covered in an employment contract include the following:

The parties involved in the contract (employer and employee).

- Duration of the job.
- Specific job duties and expectations.
- Detailed compensation and benefits offerings.
- Conditions of employment.
- Grounds for termination or resignation.
- Noncompete agreements, including nonsolicitation of current employees.
- Intellectual property components.

A generic offer letter that has a standard format can be used for most positions. The standard form would allow for the insertion of the applicable position; the Fair Labor Standards Act exemption status; start date; full- or part-time status and rates of pay, expressed in weekly or monthly terms; reporting relationships; and the at-will statement. First, carefully check state law relative to employment at will, as some states (notably Montana) do not recognize at-will employment.

As with any document, it is imperative that an offer letter template is reviewed by legal counsel to ensure that it meets legal requirements and truly does not give the appearance of an employment contract.

Chapter 6
Hiring Decisions

Q: Are there regulations that require a company to post open positions, either internally or externally? If so, is there a requirement on the length of time for the internal posting?

Only federal contractors obligated under the Vietnam Era Veterans' Readjustment Assistance Act (VEVRAA), as amended by the Jobs for Veterans Act (JVA), are required by regulation to post open positions. To implement the affirmative action requirement, check VEVRAA and its implementation regulations found at 41 C.F.R. Parts 60-250[1] and 60-300,[2] which require contractors and subcontractors to list most employment openings with an appropriate employment service delivery system. Each of those delivery systems must also provide protected veterans priority referrals to such openings. Executive and top management positions, positions that will be filled from within the contractor's organization, and positions lasting three days or less are exempt from this mandatory job listing requirement. Listing employment openings with the state workforce agency job bank or with the local employment service delivery system when the opening occurs will satisfy the requirement to list jobs with the local employment service delivery system. Although there is no specific duration a job must be posted, the general rule is that contractors must list employment openings with the appropriate employment delivery system concurrently with a contractor's use of any other recruitment source or effort.

Typically, job vacancy announcements include an opening and closing date for applicants to submit expressions of interest. In these cases, a contractor should list employment openings for such positions as often as the contractor considers individuals for a particular position. For example, a contractor may routinely hire engineers and keep each vacancy announcement open for 15 days on a rolling basis. Subsequently, the contractor should list the engineer employment opening every 15 days with the appropriate employment delivery system.

Alternatively, a contractor should list employment openings at least as frequently as the time period used by the employment delivery system to maintain an active listing. For example, if an employment delivery system keeps job listings active for only 30 days, a contractor that is continually accepting applications for a particular position should list the employment opening every 30 days.

Employers not obligated under VEVRAA or JVA may still have affirmative action plans (AAPs), and within those plans, the employer will likely set forth the organization's rules on job postings. These self-imposed rules must be followed for the organization to be in compliance with its own AAP.

Employers with collective bargaining agreements (CBAs) may have bargained job posting procedures, especially as they relate to internal postings and advancement opportunities. If so, these rules must be followed to be in compliance with the CBA.

Other employers may have their own internal and external recruiting policies and practices, which become the "laws" that should be followed consistently. Posting or not posting and for how long is entirely up to these employers, and their intentions should be made clear within their policies for their best protection.

Q: What is the difference between equal employment opportunity, affirmative action, and diversity? What is the

difference between disparate impact and disparate treatment?

Equal employment opportunity (EEO) means freedom from discrimination on the basis of sex, color, religion, national origin, disability, and age. EEO rights are guaranteed by federal and state fair employment laws and are enforced by the U.S. Equal Employment Opportunity Commission (EEOC) and its state counterparts.

Affirmative action plans (AAPs) define an employer's standard for proactively recruiting, hiring, and promoting women, minorities, individuals with disabilities, and veterans. Affirmative action is deemed a moral and social obligation to amend historical wrongs and eliminate the present effects of past discrimination. AAPs include numerical measures with the intent of increasing the representation of minorities. Federal contractors above certain dollar limits are required to institute AAPs under Executive Order 11246 and its regulations.[3] The Office of Federal Contract Compliance Programs is charged with enforcing contractor affirmative action mandates. Without violating Title VII of the Civil Rights Act, other employers may institute voluntary AAPs to remedy past discrimination if certain conditions are met. These are set forth in EEOC guidance on the subject.

Diversity initiatives are goals devised to measure acceptance of minorities by embracing cultural differences within the workplace. Diversity initiatives are twofold: valuing diversity and managing diversity. The value of diversity is achieved through awareness, education, and positive recognition of cultural differences within the workplace. The management of diversity expounds on the experience and establishes the business case for diversity that is closely aligned with an employer's organizational goals.

Disparate impact refers to policies, practices, rules, or other systems that appear to be neutral but that result in a disproportionate impact on protected groups. Disparate treatment is intentional.

For example, testing a particular skill of African-Americans only is disparate treatment. Testing all applicants and getting results from that test that eliminate African-Americans disproportionately is disparate impact.

Title VII prohibits intentional discrimination based on race, color, religion, sex, or national origin and prohibits both disparate treatment and disparate impact discrimination.

In cases of disparate treatment, employees or applicants must show that intentional discriminatory practices took place. In response, an employer must show a legitimate reason for the practice.

Q: Are all employers with 15 or more employees required to follow the Uniform Guidelines on Employee Selection Procedures, including adverse impact testing and applicant tracking?

Although the Uniform Guidelines on Employee Selection Procedures (UGESP)[4] apply to federal employers and private and public employers subject to Title VII of the Civil Rights Act (that is, those with 15 or more employees), they are guidelines—not law. This means should a covered employer find itself in court on a discrimination claim, the court will apply the standards found in the UGESP to determine whether unlawful discrimination has occurred. Therefore, an employer that has followed the guidelines, including applicant tracking and adverse impact testing, will most likely have a strong, albeit not guaranteed, defense.

The guidelines were issued in 1978 by federal agencies trying to establish a course for employers to follow to ensure they were using nondiscriminatory employment practices to be compliant under Title VII. At that time, civil rights laws were still fairly new, and employers needed clear guidance on how to revise or review their long-standing selection practices to ensure compliance under the new law. The guidelines are a roadmap, based on prior court decisions, to help an employer not only to develop lawful hiring and promotion practices but also to defend itself successfully in court if sued for discrimination on the basis of race, color, religion, sex, or national origin. The guidelines also serve as a unified stance for all federal agencies to work from. They apply to all aspects of selection, including testing, educational requirements, physical requirements, and evaluations of work samples or performance, to name a few broad categories.

The UGESP endeavors to help employers either avoid adverse impact during selection or show that any resulting adverse impact is based on a validated selection method. The guidelines provide detailed guidance on validation testing methods, suggesting content, construct, and criterion-related validity are the acceptable methods to consider.

Applicant tracking records are to be kept only by sex, race, and national origin. This can be done by visual observation, personal knowledge, or self-identification. If using self-identification forms, the employer should ensure the applicant understands this information will not be used in making a hiring decision but is being requested to comply with federal record-keeping guidelines. This information should be kept separately from the application and personnel folder.

Q: May a religious institution give preference to hiring adherents of the same religion? What is a ministerial exception under Title VII?

Title VII of the Civil Rights Act makes it unlawful for an employer "to fail or refuse to hire or to discharge any individual, or otherwise to discriminate against any individual with respect to his compensation, terms, conditions, or privileges of employment"[5] because of the individual's religion. However, Title VII includes an exception for defined "religious organizations" and "religious educational institutions."[6]

Under the exception, religious organizations are permitted to give employment preference to adherents of the same religion. This applies only to those institutions whose "purpose and character are primarily religious."[7] In determining whether an entity is religious, considerations include whether its articles of incorporation state a religious purpose and whether its day-to-day operations are religious. For example, are the services it performs, the product it produces, or the educational curriculum it provides directed toward propagation of the religion? Another consideration is whether it is nonprofit and if it is affiliated with, or supported by, a church or other religious organization.

Religious organizations may not otherwise discriminate in employment on the basis of race, color, national origin, sex, age, or disability. Thus, a religious organization is not permitted to engage in racially discriminatory hiring by claiming that its religious beliefs include not associating with people of other races. And, though Title VII does not expressly exempt religious organizations from provisions barring discrimination on the basis of race, gender, or national origin, there is a limited "ministerial exception" that allows religious employers to avoid liability for discrimination claims from employees who qualify as "ministers."[8]

The U.S. Supreme Court has ruled that workplace bias lawsuits may not be brought by church employees who act as ministers to their denominations.[9] The high court explicitly recognized—for the first time—a ministerial exception to federal, state, and local laws against discrimination on the job. The ministerial exception comes from the First Amendment principle that government regulation of church administration, including the appointment of clergy, impedes the free exercise of religion and constitutes impermissible government entanglement with church authority.

Religious organizations should keep in mind that, despite the Supreme Court's ruling, they may face significant litigation in trying to determine the reach of the ministerial exception when applied to teachers and other lay employees, given that the high court failed to provide a bright-line test to determine who qualifies as a minister.

Q: Can a company refuse to hire individuals who smoke?

Though individuals who smoke have no constitutional right to smoke or federal employment law protection, some states prohibit discrimination based on legal, off-duty activities. And several states go as far as to specifically prohibit employers from making complete abstinence from smoking a condition of employment.

Once the employer has confirmed there is no state employment law prohibition against no-smoker hiring policies, the employer will want to consider the advantages and disadvantages of such a policy.

Some of the potential advantages include improved morale of nonsmokers, better air quality, lower building maintenance fees, decreased health care claims or premiums, and lower premiums for fire and casualty insurance.

Some of the disadvantages include a more limited pool of qualified job applicants, difficulty in monitoring employees' after-hours activities, and employers' increased exposure to lawsuits for discrimination and invasion of privacy.

Employers that cannot or choose not to implement a preferential hiring policy may consider a smoke-free workplace policy as an alternative. At minimum, a smoke-free workplace reduces the employer's liability for lawsuits by nonsmokers (for exposure to secondhand smoke) and could reduce the employer's building maintenance and insurance expenses.

As with any new policy consideration, the employer is encouraged to consult legal counsel prior to policy implementation. The employer should ensure the policy is properly communicated and administered consistently without regard to the applicants' race, sex, national origin, age, or religion.

Q: What should an employer tell a candidate who is not selected for the position?

There are many schools of thought on this issue, and good advice can vary widely between internal and external candidates, those only making the first cut or those considered final candidates, and even the level of the position. Internal candidates should be informed in person and given actionable items on which to improve, but deciding how to inform external candidates can be more challenging. Certainly, a company's reputation is at stake because the manner in which an organization handles applicants reflects how it treats its employees. Given that a negative applicant experience could turn off both future applicants and customers, employers should respond in a professional manner to all applicants, thank them for applying, and do so in a timely manner. In most cases, applicants have put forth a great deal of effort in researching the organization, crafting their resume and cover letter, and getting family and friends to review it, so they will be optimistically waiting to hear from prospective employers. No response at all is frustrating and disheartening and can result in a negative perception of the organization.

In terms of exactly what to say, there are pros and cons to both options discussed below. Employers should work with their executives and even legal counsel to determine the best approach for their organization.

Employers may choose to give a neutral, nonspecific reason to a candidate not selected for the position. This option entails a standard response such as "Thank you for applying, but we have decided to pursue other applicants," or some variation thereof. This is a popular option for several reasons: It is easy to be consistent, it does not open itself up to arguments from the applicant, and it stops human resources from being a career counselor to a host of applicants. Attorneys often like this approach as well because inadvertent, unlawfully discriminatory statements cannot be made. If an applicant persists to know a reason for the rejection or becomes angry, human resources can simply reiterate the response and end the conversation.

The employer could decide to state a specific reason or coach the applicant. This response could entail everything from "You were chewing gum and texting during the interview" to "Your responses to several interview questions did not showcase the leadership capabilities we are looking for." Although this approach can be helpful, especially for younger workers with limited interviewing skills, it can also backfire on the employer when the applicant chooses to debate the employer's reasoning and tries to get the employer to change its mind. The employer's intention is good: trying to help candidates in their next interview, giving them more specific closure, and imparting an honest and thoughtful image of the employer. But caution is warranted with this approach. Some applicants may be grateful for the feedback, but others may feel they were unfairly denied employment and may start an argument with the employer or may begin to feel litigious.

Q: What should HR consider when rehiring employees?

As the economy improves and employers consider whether to rehire laid-off employees or those who left voluntarily, HR professionals must have a plan to ensure that hiring is done fairly and consistently in compliance with company policy and employment laws. Without a rehire plan, organizations could be at risk of charges that rehiring was unfair or unlawfully discriminatory.

Rehiring workers has a number of benefits:

- Former employees are known commodities and are typically less expensive to onboard than brand-new employees.

- Recruiting from a potential rehire list can be less expensive than having to advertise, which is often a large part of a company's recruiting budget.
- Former employees often bring competitive intelligence and a broader knowledge of the market.
- Rehires may be instrumental in helping develop newer workers because they can act as mentors for recruits who are new to the scene.
- Former employees may require less retraining because of reduced learning curves.
- They are familiar with the company's culture, mission, and vision.

Unless there is a collective bargaining agreement in place, there is generally not a legal requirement for a company to rehire former employees, even after a layoff. Therefore, it is a strategic decision for an organization to make.

HR professionals should, however, keep in mind that if a company rehires too quickly after a layoff, it runs a greater risk of the validity of the layoff being questioned, and of concerns being raised that the layoff is just a pretext for unlawful discrimination. HR should be able to clearly articulate the business reason for rehiring.

In addition, a clearly written, communicated, and followed policy about recruiting employees for rehire is in an employer's best interests. Such a policy will eliminate confusion and could serve as a defense if a discrimination charge is filed. It is also important to include a clear definition of the term rehire, including whether a rehire is able to keep his or her previously earned paid time off, eligibility for company 401(k) and pension plan, and seniority. It is generally considered a good practice to have all new-hire paperwork completed to ensure proper compliance with the W-4, the I-9, and any other required documents.

Chapter 7

Interviewing

Q: Can a recruiter ask a candidate, "Do you own a car?"

The question of whether an individual owns a car is irrelevant, unless the position requires an employee to use his or her personal vehicle to travel between worksites, or other locations, as a primary job duty.

Whether candidates use public transportation, bike, carpool, or drive to work really has no bearing on how they will perform in the job. Therefore, the mode of transportation used to get to work is not what an employer should be considering when making a selection decision.

A recruiter's asking an applicant "Do you have a car?" often intends to find out if this person will have attendance issues. An applicant's ability to be at work on time every day definitely is a job-related concern. But the question the recruiter asked does not obtain the information he or she was seeking.

When employers develop interview questions, they should think about what kind of answers they may receive when asking each question. Avoid questions that have more to do with personal lifestyles than with job experience. Phrase the question so that the answer will describe on-the-job qualities instead of personal qualities, and if the question is not related to performance on the job, it should not be asked.

Below are a few sample questions that may help assess if an applicant has outside commitments or transportation issues, which could negatively affect his or her attendance at work. Choose questions that best reflect the company's hours of work, overtime, and attendance policies.

- Do you have reliable transportation to and from work?
- What shifts or days are you available to work?
- Our second shift is from 2 p.m. to 10 p.m. Monday through Friday. Are you available to work this shift every weekday?
- We do have a mandatory overtime policy. Required overtime could extend your workday to 10-hour days or may require working on Saturdays as needed. Are you available to work this type of overtime schedule?
- Do you foresee any problems with working a third shift schedule?
- When overtime is required, will transportation be a problem?

Q: Is there a problem with writing notes directly on applications or resumes?

Many experts advise employers to avoid the practice of writing notes on applications or resumes. The reason behind this recommendation is that notes an employer makes on an application or resume might be used to support an applicant's claim of discrimination. Also, handwritten notes on a handwritten application may make it appear that the employer was trying to sabotage the application in some way. Notes that are relevant to an applicant's skills or experience and that are related to the job in question can be recorded on a separate interview evaluation sheet to accomplish the same goal of accurately recording information from an interview.

Q: What are some tips for screening resumes?

Screening a stack of resumes can be a daunting task for even experienced recruiters. However, with a little prework and an organized approach, the process can be streamlined to help select the best candidates to interview.

HR professionals should know the organization's positions and vacancies. They should be familiar with each open job and its position description to efficiently and accurately compare the experiences listed on resumes with the requirements of the job description. HR professionals may want to ensure the following:

- That the job descriptions (especially for vacancies) are up to date. HR staff may want to meet with hiring managers to make sure any duties, skills, or credentials that may have changed have been included or removed as necessary.
- That if a job description is significantly out of date, a job analysis will be performed to obtain an accurate description to ensure a proper hire.
- That the qualities a person needs to ensure success in the position—such as the ability to work independently, being results-oriented, or having strong teamwork skills—have been identified.

An evaluation grid created in a spreadsheet can help organize the resumes. HR staff can chart and rate the resumes as they come in. This chart may be altered for different positions. Some ideas for creating the grid include the following:

- Listing the resumes alphabetically (by name) or numerically (in order received) along the Y-axis (down the column on the left).
- Listing the qualifications to consider along the X axis (across the row at the top). Included should be such headings as credentials, competencies (SHRM's sample interview questions[1] can provide guidance to help identify competencies needed for the position), educational requirements, certifications, years of experience, supervisory experience, accomplishments, relocation needed, gaps in employment, and spelling/grammar errors. The heading categories that are "must-haves"

for the candidate to be considered for the position should be identified.

As the resumes are charted on the evaluation grid, they can be organized into three folders as follows:
- Yes: meets all criteria.
- No: does not meet must-have or minimum criteria.
- Maybe: meets must-have criteria and some additional criteria, but not all.

After the resumes have been placed in the folders, the HR department should review each placement to ensure the "no's" really do not meet minimum requirements and the "maybe's" do not belong in one of the other two folders; resumes reviewed early in the process might have been misclassified. Next, the final "yes" folder can be reviewed for more specific information. For instance:
- Are there actual accomplishments to support the competencies required?
- Does the resume include statements like "reduced unemployment claims by 12 percent" or "increased productivity by 5 percent" when "results-driven" is a competency for the position?
- If job-hopping is common for the industry, does the applicant's job history indicate movement that exceeds the norm?
- Are there any unacceptable writing or style errors?
- Are there any unexplained gaps in employment?
- Is the explanation acceptable?

Based on the answers to these questions, the final folders can be sorted. The questionable resumes can move into the "maybe" or "no" files as warranted. The remaining resumes can be placed in the "yes" folder in the order of those with the most positive answers on top, followed by those that may be more questionable, but are still acceptable. Applicants whose resumes are at the top of the pile should be interviewed first, followed by the remainder of the "yes" folder if more interviews are desired.

Q: When would an employer use a group interview technique?

Group interviews have become increasingly popular among employers. To determine if a group interview is right for the organization, an employer needs to understand the basic group interview techniques, the benefits associated with the group interview, and the best time to use a group interview. A group interview is an interview technique in which several candidates are interviewed simultaneously for similar positions. To be successful, group interviews must be well planned and executed. When deciding to employ a group interview, organizations need to devise a plan that outlines the company objectives and purpose for using a group interview strategy.

Generally, the interviewer poses hypothetical problems to the group, as well as provides group activities that require the candidates to work as a team to find a solution. This approach allows the interviewer to observe the candidates' interactions with each other and how well they work as a team. Group questions allow an interviewer to observe the candidates' "soft skills" such as teamwork, problem-solving, and interpersonal communication. Additionally, the interviewer incorporates individual questions for each candidate. The use of both group questions and individual questions not only allows the candidates to articulate how they would handle possible situations, but also allows the employer to see each candidate in action.

Group interviews are best used by employers that need to find a large number of employees quickly—for example, start-up companies that need a large number of employees to open the business.

This technique allows the employer the opportunity to screen a number of candidates at one time, reducing the interview process. Group interviews are most effective when hiring for positions that require excellent people skills, especially when the job regularly deals with consumers or the public. Group interviews are also effective when teamwork is an integral part of the job. The group interview allows an employer to observe behaviors that are reflective of success on the job before the employer actually invests time and money into hiring a candidate.

Interviewing multiple candidates one-on-one may cause the interviewer to blur and intertwine the candidates' knowledge and experience so that the ideal candidate may not be selected. However, group interviews certainly save time, and could reduce turnover, which saves the organization money too. Understanding the company's objectives and determining if group interviews are right for the employer could be a successful technique if used in certain situations, or to gain insight on specific behaviors that are more effectively visible during active involvement in a group setting or activity.

Q: How should an employer interview applicants with disabilities?

The job interview plays a critical role in the hiring process, allowing an employer the opportunity to identify the individual who possesses the best mix of knowledge, skills, and abilities (KSAs) for the position available. Below is information that may assist employers in ensuring maximum benefit from an interview when the person being interviewed has a disability.

Preparing for the Interview

When preparing for an interview with an applicant with a disability, HR professionals should:

- Ensure that their company's application and interviewing procedures comply with the Americans with Disabilities Act (ADA) and the Americans with Disabilities Act Amendments Act, which prohibit asking disability-related questions before a job offer is made.
- Check that their application forms, employment offices, and interviewing locations are accessible to persons with a variety of disabilities.
- Be willing to make appropriate and reasonable accommodations to enable an applicant with a disability to participate in the interview, explaining ahead of time what is involved in the process. For example, if an applicant who is blind states that he or she will need help completing forms, that assistance should be provided. Employers can offer an interpreter or other assistance that is reasonable for an applicant who is deaf and requests assistance in communicating. For applicants with cognitive disabilities, details or specific instructions can be provided, if such accommodation is required.
- Inform applicants ahead of time if they will be required to take a test to demonstrate their ability to perform actual or simulated tasks so that they can request a reasonable accommodation, such as a different format for a written test, if necessary. (Such tests are permitted under the ADA as long as they are uniformly given to all applicants.)

Conducting the Interview

Interviewers can help ensure a successful interview experience by doing the following:

- Relaxing, and making the applicant feel relaxed. If the applicant has a visible disability or reveals a disability during the interview, the interviewer should concentrate on the individual, not on the disability.

- Treating the individual with the same respect shown any candidate whose skills are being sought. Likewise, individuals with disabilities should be held to the same standards as all applicants.
- Asking only job-related questions that speak to the functions of the job for which the applicant is applying.
- Concentrating on the applicant's technical and professional KSAs, experiences, and interests.
- Not trying to imagine how they would perform a specific job if they had the applicant's disability. The applicant has mastered alternate ways of living and working. If the applicant has a known disability, either because it is obvious or was revealed by the applicant, interviewers may ask the applicant to describe how he or she would perform the job.

Medical examinations are prohibited under the ADA prior to making an offer. However, a job offer may be conditional based on the results of a medical examination if all employees entering similar jobs are also required to take an examination. If, after the medical examination, the employer decides not to hire an individual because of a disability, the employer must demonstrate that the reason for the rejection is job-related and consistent with business necessity.

Chapter 8
Management and Communication

Q: When should a worker be classified as part time or full time?

When a part-time employee has been consistently working on a full-time basis, an employer cannot overlook the need to reevaluate the employee's status. Although laws do not dictate how an employer defines part-time and full-time status internally, if such definitions deny employees benefits they are eligible for, serious legal implications can result. Timely evaluation and reclassification to a full-time status when appropriate can eliminate these risks.

Some laws, such as the Patient Protection and Affordable Care Act, COBRA, and other federal and state employment laws, may define part-time and full-time employment for compliance with that particular law. But how an employer chooses to define part-time and full-time employment internally is up to the employer. An employee's classification as full time or part time has an impact on an employer's benefits offerings such as health and welfare plans governed by the Employee Retirement Income Security Act (ERISA) and Internal Revenue Service (IRS) regulations. For example, most employer health care plans have eligibility requirements that typically state something like "all full-time employees working 35 hours or more per week are eligible to participate in the plan." When a part-time employee consistently works 35 hours per week, a problem arises if this employee is denied benefits based on his or her part-time classification. The U.S. Department of Labor and the IRS would likely agree that an employee consistently working 35 hours per week is a full-time employee. Therefore, when eligible employees are not being offered participation in benefits plans, it can lead to ERISA and IRS violations and could jeopardize the tax qualification of the entire plan.

But what does "consistently working" mean, and how often should an employer evaluate a part-time employee's classification? Again, this decision is largely up to the employer, but working with legal counsel to determine a reasonable standard for full- and part-time classification would be wise. Considerations include the following:

- Is there an end date to the extended hours? Perhaps the employee is filling in for an employee on short-term leave or helping on a project with a certain deadline not too far in the future. If so, this may help defend the employer's stance that the employee is not a full-time employee.
- Are the extended hours seasonal, increasing during busy times of the year? Perhaps the employer can incorporate this information in its definition of part time, including a limitation on the number of weeks such extra hours may be worked per year, and monitor it closely.

Perhaps just defining "consistently" as 30, 60, or 90 days, and reevaluating classification at that time, would work best for the employer.

Whatever reasonable standard employers choose, this decision should be reflected in company policies and benefits plans as appropriate. The standard must be followed consistently, and part-time status evaluations should be ongoing.

Q: What factors should determine how many direct reports a manager has?

The number of direct reports a manager has is referred to as his or her "span of control." The ideal number of direct reports who can be managed effectively can be elusive, though research and theories do exist.[1] Although no perfect ratio likely exists, span of control is critical in understanding organizational design and the behaviors within an organization, such as the approach used to interact with employees and the effectiveness of communication between each level within an organization. Therefore, many factors need to be evaluated before determining the best ratio within an organization.

In terms of organizational design, a small number of direct reports creates a narrow span of control and a hierarchical structure, also known as a "tall" organization. Narrow spans of control are more expensive for organizations, but they allow managers to have more time with direct reports, and they tend to spark professional growth and advancement. In contrast, a wide span of control refers to a larger number of direct reports supervised by one manager, creating a "flat" organization. This approach increases the number of interactions between the manager and his or her direct reports, which could cause managers to become overwhelmed but can also provide more autonomy to employees.

Some key factors to review when determining the appropriate span of control within an organization include the following:

- Organizational size. Large organizations tend to have a narrow span of control, whereas smaller organizations often have a wider span of control. This difference is usually due to the costs involved with more managers and the financial resources available to an organization. Communication may be slower with narrow spans if it must pass through several levels of management.
- Workforce skill level. The complexity or simplicity of the tasks performed by the employees affects the number of desirable direct reports. Generally, routine tasks involving repetition require less supervisory control of a manager, allowing

a wider span of control, whereas complex tasks or dynamic workplace conditions may be best suited for a narrower span of control, where managers can provide more individualized attention.

- Organizational culture. Organizations need to determine the desired culture when designing their span of control. Flexible workplaces usually have a wider span of control because employees are given more autonomy and flexibility in the production of their work.
- Manager's responsibilities. Employers should review whether the organizational expectations allow the managers to be effective with the number of direct reports they have, especially related to individual responsibilities, departmental planning, and training. For instance, executives often have fewer direct reports than other managers in the organization.

Q: What are the advantages of cafeteria-style relocation programs?

Cafeteria-style relocation programs differ from the more traditional, tiered programs in their flexibility, cost control methods, and ability to provide a more creative approach to traditional programs. A successful relocation program is a cost-effective program that will ultimately attract the best candidates for a position and facilitate current employees to move where the business needs them. Though traditional, tiered programs are often based strictly on job level with a finite set of benefits, cafeteria-style relocation programs may be an option to tailor to the needs of the individual while still maintaining budget controls and core benefits.

Flexibility is the major advantage of cafeteria-style programs, considering there are many types of relocation situations, from domestic to global, single to family, and young professional to senior management. For example, some employees may need home sale or home purchase assistance, with strong spousal and child support services, whereas others may need only adequate housing allowances and light shipment of household goods. In the case of global assignments, employees may prefer intense language training and cultural training services. Tailoring the package in a more flexible way can increase employee satisfaction and acceptance of relocations and result in more successful talent management.

Control of the budget is a major concern, and stringent cost-cutting can leave programs too limited to achieve the desired results. Employees and potential employees will not see the value in moving if their own needs are not met. Therefore, flexibility in the benefits offered can address the real needs of those relocating and reduce costs by eliminating benefits that are not important to individual movers. To keep costs under control, caps are typically placed on the value of selection options and depend on both the job level of employees and the type of business assignment. Generally, a core benefits package (for example, travel costs to the destination, temporary housing, and transportation of household goods) is applied to all relocating employees, coupled with flexible elements (for example, home sale, home purchase, dependent support, advanced language training, and settling-in services) tailored to the type of employee or relocation situation. This approach results in a budget-friendly yet highly tailored benefit. It balances employee's needs with the employer's ability to keep a cost-effective program.

Employers can also consider a hybrid program to provide a tiered approach, which addresses more benefits for higher-level employees or international employees, but builds in the flexibility among the tiers allowing choice and personalization. The cafeteria-style options can minimize costs and enable the employer to address or limit the need for exceptions, which could otherwise be costly. Variations in the model can still be a cost-effective option and still meet organizational goals to attract, retain, and relocate talent as needed.

Q: What is an effective practice for announcing new hires?

Communication of new hires should be announced in a way that fits a company's culture. In small organizations, face-to-face introductions may be most appropriate. But in most larger organizations, e-mail, company newsletters, or bulletin boards in break areas are used as the primary method of company communications, and therefore are also appropriate for new hire announcements.

Announcements should include the new hire's name, job title, start date, and manager's name. If it is a new position in the organization, this is a good time to share a brief description of the job duties. Sharing the new hire's contact information, such as phone extension and e-mail address, is also helpful.

Many employers like to include personal information in announcements. Co-workers are interested in the background of a new hire, and this information may help build connections among colleagues. Before an organization includes personal information such as work history, educational history, hobbies, or favorite activities, the new hire should have an opportunity to provide the information he or she wishes to add or to review the announcement prior to sending it out.

When determining who should sign or send out a new hire announcement, the employer should select the person who has had the most interaction with the new employee during the hiring process. This is usually the hiring manager. An announcement from this person makes it a more personalized experience for the new hire. For consistency, many employers have announcements come from the company president, human resources, or the department head.

Chapter 9
Pre-employment Testing

Q: What compliance issues are involved in creating a pre-employment test?

Pre-employment testing must adhere to the employment provisions of the Americans with Disabilities Act. If a test screens out or tends to screen out a person with a disability, the test must be job-related and must be consistent with business necessity. Even if a test is job-related and justified by business necessity, an employer has an obligation to provide a specific reasonable accommodation, if necessary. The reasonable accommodation obligation applies to testing by protecting persons with disabilities from being excluded from jobs that they actually can do, because a disability either prevents them from taking a test or negatively influences a test result. However, an employer does not need to provide an alternative test format for a person with an impaired skill if the purpose of the test is to measure that skill.

Employers are encouraged to check their state laws before implementing a pre-employment testing program. If a testing program involves medical examinations, AIDS testing, or genetic testing, other rules and regulations govern those types of tests.

Q: What do we need to do to implement a pre-employment drug screening?

The design and implementation of a pre-employment drug screening program should involve the input and cooperation of human resources, legal counsel, and security. The policy for testing should comply with the drug testing laws in the state in which the test is given.

The requirements of relevant laws should be incorporated into the program. Local and state laws, in addition to federal laws, may need to be reviewed. Federal laws that may be applicable include the following:

- The Omnibus Transportation Employee Testing Act. This law mandates pre-employment testing. Employers in the transportation industry should review this legislation for procedural requirements.
- The U.S. Department of Defense. This federal agency specifies drug-free workplace requirements for its contractors.
- Executive Order 12564.[1] This order establishes drug testing policies and procedures for federal employees.
- The Americans with Disabilities Act (ADA). This law allows pre-offer tests for illegal substances; however, only post-offer tests for blood alcohol level are permitted. In addition, the ADA protects applicants who have successfully completed a drug rehabilitation program. Therefore, an employer should establish a time frame within which an applicant who previously tested positive can reapply.
- The Rehabilitation Act. This law applies to the federal government, government contractors, and those receiving financial assistance from the federal government. The act protects those in drug rehabilitation programs or those who have successfully completed such programs.

The types of substances to screen for and the acceptable level of use should be identified. Legal requirements pertaining to the screening of the substances should also be identified.

Employers should determine whether urine or blood sampling will be used. Urine sampling requires the establishment of procedures to prevent substitution or debasing of the sample by the addition of foreign materials.

The privacy of samples should be maintained by establishing a sample identification method that does not include the applicant's name. In addition, a sound chain-of-custody procedure must be used.

When selecting a lab to conduct the testing, employers should choose one that meets their testing needs. In addition employers should do the following:

- Confirm that the lab has a history of highly reliable results and a methodology to confirm initial positive results. Gas chromatography or mass spectrometry are reliable methods for verification. Also, the lab should be enrolled in a minimum of one independently administered program to monitor its success rate.
- Check whether the lab is licensed and accredited per applicable local, state, and federal laws.
- Determine the complete services provided and the associated fees so that testing costs can be determined.
- Set up a procedure to frequently check the quality of service provided by the lab.
- Place a notice of the substance-screening policy on employment applications. Employers should notify the applicant of the testing procedure and test the applicant only after he or she has been notified of the test and procedures and has given his or her consent. All applicants for all jobs should be tested.
- Give employees an opportunity to retest, as well as a means to challenge results. The consequences of a positive test result should be made clear to the applicant.

Q: What are the compliance issues involved in conducting pre-employment physical examinations?

The law that most affects an employer's ability to require pre-employment physical examinations is the Americans with Disabilities Act (ADA). Essentially, an employer may require a physical examination only after a contingent offer of employment has been made. No physical examination can be required before an offer is made. Physical examinations can be required only if the following conditions exist:

- All other candidates in the job category are also required to have a physical examination.
- The candidate's medical history is treated confidentially and is kept separate from other employment-related records.
- The results of the examination are not used to discriminate against persons covered by the ADA.

A physical exam should assess whether the person is currently able to perform the duties of a job with or without accommodation. To make this assessment, the medical practitioner who conducts the examination must have a clear understanding of the job. The medical practitioner assumes no responsibility for the ultimate hiring decision. Also, it is wise to have only job-related physical attributes or conditions examined.

Contingent offers of employment may be withdrawn based on the results of a physical examination if the reason for withdrawing the offer is job-related, is consistent with business necessity, or is imperative to avoid a direct threat to health or safety. Contingent offers may also be withdrawn (a) if there is no reasonable accommodation that the employer could make to allow the person to perform the job, or (b) if providing the needed accommodation would cause undue hardship. Offers of employment cannot be legally withdrawn because of speculation about a person's future attendance or use of benefits.

Q: How should a company implement a pre-employment testing program?

Pre-employment testing is a selection tool that can provide valuable information to aid the selection process. Pre-employment tests can add objectivity to the selection process if applicants for the same position take the same test under the same conditions and if the test accurately measures skills essential to job performance. Pre-employment tests should be validated (content validity, construct validity, criterion-related validity) to ensure that they measure the knowledge or skills that an applicant would need to perform the job.

Many compliance issues should be considered when implementing a pre-employment testing program. The Uniform Guidelines on Employee Selection Procedures (UGESP) is one tool that can help with compliance issues.[2] The UGESP sets forth a single set of employment standards on all employers covered under Title VII of the Civil Rights Act or Executive Order 11246,[3] and they aid in determining whether an employer policy or practice causes a "disproportionate adverse impact" on the employment opportunities of any race, sex, or ethnic group. To determine whether a selection procedure causes an adverse impact, employers should apply the "4/5ths rule" or 80 percent rule. The 80 percent rule involves comparing the hiring rates for different groups. If the selection rate for a protected group (defined by race, ethnic origin, sex, etc.) is less than 4/5ths (or 80 percent) of that for the group with the highest selection rate, the procedure is considered discriminatory.

Chapter 10
Recruiting

Q: Can an employer skip the recruiting process, including job posting, if it has already identified a candidate it wants to hire or promote?

Employers may legally skip the recruiting process, but it is not always a good idea. Lack of consistent application of any policy could lead to potential unlawful discrimination practices and should be avoided where possible.

Federal contractors required by regulation to post jobs are not able to skip the recruiting process and must follow their normal procedures.

Other employers with affirmative action plans or collective bargaining agreements that set forth a recruitment and posting practice must also follow their own guidelines, or they could violate their own plans and agreements.

Employers with recruiting and job posting policies should also follow their normal procedures, unless their policy indicates the procedures can be changed at the discretion of the employer, such as when an internal successor is identified or as best meeting the business needs.

In general, when making exceptions to recruiting policies, the employer should be able to support the business need behind the exception. Without such support, an employer is best protected against potential unlawful discrimination claims by consistently applying its policies or practices.

Q: Can a company advertise for candidates with the requirement that they must currently be employed?

Even in the absence of current federal law barring discrimination against the unemployed, employers should proceed cautiously in excluding those not working from job applicant pools. Title VII of the Civil Rights Act protects individuals from employment discrimination based on race, ethnicity, religion, gender, disability, age, national origin, and veteran status. Even though unemployed persons are not a protected class under federal law, an ad of this type might arguably give rise to a claim of disparate impact. For example, if a particular applicant market had a disproportionate number of minorities who are out of work compared to nonminorities, restricting the pool to employed individuals could have a disparate impact on minority applicants.

Many employers claim a legitimate business reason for having a policy of filling open positions with only those who already are employed, particularly in high-tech industries. If someone has been out of work for a year, that person might not have the skills necessary for a particular job, such as being well versed with particular technology or equipment.

Although this advertising is drawing attention from the media, it may not be the attention an organization is seeking, and it can cause job seekers to question the ethical nature of the employer. In this age of uncertain job prospects, applicants are looking for employers with a heart and may be more likely to pass on jobs with companies that have the perception of not caring for their employees and the community around them.

A recruiter's goal for an organization is to hire the best person to do the job. By skipping over the unemployed, some of the most viable candidates might be overlooked, especially with the current historic unemployment rates. In today's uncertain economy, even outstanding, dedicated, and loyal employees are being laid off.

When hiring, it is always best to focus on the skills, education, and experience necessary to perform the job. Excluding a candidate for a personal reason or for something not job-related is generally considered poor practice. And though employers are certainly encouraged to investigate a potential employee's background and past employment, it may not be a good practice to deny employment opportunities to individuals based on their current employment status.

Chapter 11

Retention, Turnover, and Onboarding

Q: How do I calculate retention? Is retention related to turnover?

Retention rate is not simply the inverse of turnover. For the experienced workforce planner, the retention rate complements the turnover rate. By calculating both the retention rate and turnover rate, a workforce planner can obtain a more complete view of worker movement than by calculating either metric alone.

By definition, the retention rate is the percentage of employees who were employed at the beginning of a period and remain with the company at the end of the period. The retention rate tracks particular employees over time and is unaffected by subsequently hired workers. This figure is quite useful, but the downside is that it does not track the departures of employees who joined and subsequently left during the period being tracked.

Turnover rate is often defined as the number of separations divided by the average number of employees during that same time period. The most common formula used to determine turnover is the number of exits divided by the number of employees for a given period.

If an employer's purpose is to compare the employer's figures to external benchmarks, many organizations using this particular benchmark often include a raw figure that includes all separations, including retirements and voluntary separations. Thus, their figures often show the total number of exits divided by the number of employees. The problem with comparisons made using this definition is that companies have no idea how many of their departures were retirements or terminations; this type of benchmark data is of limited value.

Organizations can use the formulas below to calculate retention rate and turnover rate.

For example, in a department of eight, two people in the department left and were replaced.

So T (turnover) = (2/8) x 100 = 25 percent

And R (retention) = (6/8) x 100 = 75 percent

However, sometimes the incumbent leaves after a short period of time and is quickly replaced. If the two positions became vacant during the time period being tracked and were filled, and those personnel were also replaced, the numbers tell a different story.

T = (4/8) x 100 = 50 percent

R = (6/8) x 100 = 75 percent

A better and more accurate metric is to track both retention and turnover.

Q: Are there any positives to turnover?

Turnover is natural and essential to the growth of any organization, and human resources can take the lead to highlight its value in more meaningful ways.

First, employers can take a closer look at what kinds of turnover their organization is experiencing—not just voluntary or involuntary, but specific categories showing both favorable and unfavorable terminations—and determine what positives can be gained from each. For example:

The case of a low-performing employee's quitting results in the following favorable possibilities:

- Reduced risk of wrongful discharge.

- Possibility to promote from within.
- Possibility to recruit for a greater skill set.
- Possible restructuring opportunities.
- Possible budget realignment opportunities.
- Possibility to increase diversity.

The case of a high-performing employee's quitting results in the following unfavorable possibilities:

- Opportunity to improve the employee development program.
- Opportunity to improve the salary/benefits plan and become more competitive.
- Opportunity to improve the diversity program.
- Opportunity to improve the performance management system and replace poor managers.

Next, a company should capture the data to show the percentage of favorable versus unfavorable turnovers and the positives associated with each for the organization as a whole or for a particular department or position. These data can be used to make action plans for improvements or to capitalize on opportunities. HR professionals should assume the lead on taking the stigma out of turnover and use it for positive organizational growth.

Certainly, high turnover is something to be concerned with, as an organization cannot move forward if it is always playing catchup with training and recruiting. Extremely low turnover can also be disconcerting—is the company stagnant? Are the employees so low performing that no one else wants to hire them? Are there no opportunities for growth and new ideas from new blood? Companies should find a middle ground that works and use the data in a way that is meaningful to their organization. Positive turnover opportunities can be tied to the mission, the budget, and the strategic plans of the organization and should not be seen as only a negative.

Q: When conducting stay interviews, how can employers mitigate trust issues employees may have with the process?

As a retention tool, many employers may consider conducting stay interviews to keep good employees from jumping ship.[1] Unlike exit interviews, which amount to autopsies of why an employee is leaving, stay interviews are conducted during employment to help employers ascertain why good employees stay and what might make them leave. It is highly recommended that managers themselves conduct these meetings, after proper training, as they have the most direct relationship with the employee.

But what if there are trust issues, either between the manager and direct report, or throughout the organization? How many employees would honestly answer the question "Have you ever thought about leaving the company?" if they felt that saying yes could make them seem less dedicated or if they feared retaliation by their manager? Managers can be trained to act ethically, but what about employee buy-in? How do employers get employees to trust the process and provide honest answers that can be acted on?

Of course, the answer is likely to be different for each employer. If a company's other data indicate that trust is a large issue for the organization, stay interviews would likely be a meaningless activity, yielding untrustworthy data that, if acted on, could prove detrimental to the employer. For these organizations, trust-building initiatives and training may be in order first, clearly showing employees that changes are afoot and that the employer is making an investment in them.

But stay interviews can actually create trust as well, so for those employers with moderate trust issues, rolling out the stay interview process with strong communications about the intent ("we value you") and how the information will be used will go a long way. By choosing less invasive questions to start with and by showing through actions how employees' responses are valued, acted on, and used positively, the employer can encourage the level of employees' trust of the process to grow. Questions like "If you suddenly came into a lot of money and decided to leave us, what would you miss most and least?" or "If you can imagine your dream job doing anything, anywhere, what would it look like?" might feel less threatening, embolden employees to open up, and give managers a chance to see what employees value in a less direct way. Once the trust levels have improved, the questions can be altered.

Additional techniques could include "rewarding" employees who have mid and top performance ratings with a stay interview, sending a clear message of their value to the company (while not creating implied contracts), or putting accountability for retention more directly onto the managers themselves, forcing them to use the information only in ethical, trustworthy ways.

Q: What is the advantage of a buddy system?

Use of a buddy system may accelerate the productivity of new hires and enhance job satisfaction so that the new employees stay with the company. Such a system helps build an immediate personal connection between the new employee and the organization. In addition, a new employee who is made to feel part of the workgroup gains more confidence and is likely to become more productive faster.

The buddy can make the new employee feel welcome, answer questions, and help the person navigate through the organization's culture. This leads the new employee to feel comfortable sooner and to achieve a sense of acceptance and belonging. For example, new hires may be uncomfortable asking questions for fear of appearing incompetent. Buddies can fill in the gap by making themselves available for questions that new hires might not want to discuss with their boss. Buddies can also show the new employees around, introduce them to others, go to lunch with them the first few days, keep lines of communication open while respecting confidentiality, and offer encouragement.

A successful buddy candidate should be a seasoned employee who has an understanding of organizational practices, culture, processes, and systems. A buddy should be a friendly volunteer with high personal performance standards, have a positive attitude, and communicate well.

The buddy's role is not to be the new employee's supervisor. Training and communicating performance standards and evaluations build a foundation for the supervisor to guide the employee in the future and should not be delegated to the buddy.

A successful buddy system includes buy-in from staff and management. The assignment should be a well-designed process with follow-through. The program should establish the following:

- Expectations for the new hire, buddy, and supervisor.
- What knowledge the buddy should impart to increase productivity and performance.
- How much time the program should take.
- Requirements for "check-ins" and follow-up from the buddy and new hire on program effectiveness.

The goal is for new employees to be acclimated to the organization quicker and become more productive sooner and to keep talent within the organization.

Chapter 12
Talent Pool

Q: What is sourcing?

Sourcing is the proactive searching for qualified job candidates for current or planned open positions; it is not the reactive function of reviewing resumes and applications sent to the company in response to a job posting or pre-screening candidates. The goal of sourcing is to collect relevant data about qualified candidates, such as names, titles, and job responsibilities.

Sourcing is typically part of the recruiting function performed by the HR professional, but it may also be conducted by managers within the company. Sourcing can identify either candidates who are not actively looking for job opportunities (passive job seekers) or candidates who are actively searching for jobs (active job seekers).

Sourcing passive job seekers can include direct calls to businesses that employ individuals who match the key requirements of the position. It can also be accomplished through networking with various business-related groups. Both passive and active job seekers can be located by sourcing job boards, social media sites, and corporate alumni associations[1] and through all types of networking.

Q: Our company would like to determine the quality of candidates in a region where we are considering opening a new office. Should we post a job ad for a position that doesn't yet exist?

Posting a job ad for nonexistent position is not a recommended practice from at least two perspectives—ethical and financial. The ethics issues raised by this practice are particularly concerning as such an action essentially amounts to misrepresentation if the company posts an advertisement for a position that it knows does not exist.

To better understand the ethics issues involved in this situation, we must first understand what is meant by the term "ethics." From an HR perspective, the Society for Human Resource Management defines ethics as "a philosophy principle concerned with opinions about appropriate and inappropriate moral conduct or behavior by an individual or social group."[2]

Ethical behavior, particularly in recruiting and hiring, is an area of responsibility for the HR function, and HR professionals should pay strict attention to adhering to ethical guidelines for this area. The rise of technology has narrowed the world, and companies are scrutinized far more closely than in the past. Therefore, an organization's reputation and how it is viewed by those inside and outside could have an impact on the company's human capital strategy.

HR professionals may want to consider doing the following:

- Looking at the consequences of their actions from the point of view of the affected person(s). Regarding the situation described above, would an HR professional want to apply for a position that the company had no intention of filling? HR staff members should ask themselves what is at stake for those involved in the process—the organization, the HR professionals, and the applicant.
- Asking if the actions truly represent the best interests of the company, and what the consequences will be if human resources goes forward with the actions. Is there another method of identifying candidates that will be more effective?
- Evaluating the situation from a financial perspective. Placing a job advertisement for a nonexistent position can be less

than cost-effective. If the company places a "blind" advertisement, the company is unlikely to attract genuinely qualified candidates. Ideal candidates may be suspicious of this type of advertisement for fear of scams, identity theft, or responding to advertisements placed by their current employer.

Some less expensive and more effective methods of determining the quality of candidates in a particular area include the following:

- Gathering demographic data—what is the educational level, cost of living, and unemployment rate in the area? The Bureau of Labor Statistics has this information available at no cost.
- Talking to the Chamber of Commerce in the area.
- Using a resume database.
- Identifying possible internal candidates.

Behaving ethically is not always easy, particularly when ethical behavior is not valued or upheld by senior management. However, for HR professionals, behaving ethically is critical to maintaining integrity and achieving success.

Q: How can sourcing give us a competitive staffing edge?

One approach to enhance an organization's recruitment and staffing speed is to change recruiter duties to include a robust sourcing dynamic. This sourcing dynamic represents the ability of the recruiter to turn one quality new hire into many by capitalizing on the organization's knowledge of the available talent through its own internal processes. An alternative for organizations is to outsource this capability to an external staffing vendor. However, for most organizations, building sourcing capability internally makes far more sense.

Recruiters need to become active partners in sourcing, to be trained in identifying sourcing opportunities, and to be charged with the responsibility for using these techniques to speed the processes in filling jobs throughout the organization.

One example where sourcing can become more robust is within the onboarding process. Recruiters should be key players in interviewing new hires to mine useful intelligence about "tag-along" candidates (others who have requisite skills and capabilities the organization needs) and glean all the information the organization needs to identify these hidden candidates when the new hire is most enthusiastic in starting his or her new job. A proficient sourcing expert will be able to obtain sufficient information on a cadre of good candidates who can be mined in accordance with the employer's hiring timetable or priorities and can focus on high-priority specialty skills needed within the organization for potential leads.

Second, if the employer has an employee referral program, this is the time to familiarize the new hire with the program and solicit referral information. Once the information has been solicited, recruiters should then update candidates' databases with this information and evaluate how best to approach candidates and when to do so.

A third sourcing opportunity lies in regular workforce planning meetings, where upcoming workforce needs for skilled candidates are identified. This is also where recruiters and managers can discuss industry expansions and contractions regarding staff ramp-ups or reductions and take advantage of opportunities where candidates can be poached. Both managers and recruiters should be charged with the task of identifying staffing trends by occupation and skills throughout the industry and providing periodic updates to senior management.

Finally, with the rise of social media, hiring managers and recruiters need to familiarize themselves with these new applications and determine how they may be applied as sourcing techniques.

As these examples show, successful sourcing requires a focus on long-term efforts to evaluate how techniques can be used to enhance an employer's staffing processes. The long-term dividends in creating a systemized approach to recruiter sourcing can be substantial, and sourcing proficiencies should be a major component of the workforce plan for a successful organization.

Q: Recruiters are calling and e-mailing our employees at work during business hours. Is this legal?

Employers on the receiving end of these calls may question the ethical nature of such a practice, but, in the United States, the practice is not illegal. It is commonly known as "poaching," a term associated with illegal hunting.

The object of "talent poachers" is to provide their clients with top talent, and, much like an endangered species, there is just not enough top talent to go around. As a result, talent poachers pursue employees who have not even expressed an interest in leaving their current employers. The talent poacher commonly contacts an employee directly at work, and if the employee is not interested, the poacher may even offer a gift for the name of another unsuspecting employee.

To prevent or discourage poaching, employers should consider removing employee contact information from company websites. Employers may also institute policies to restrict nonbusiness communications during work hours and should remind employees of company communication monitoring policies. Employers may also consider using noncompete agreements to prohibit employees, especially those with access to confidential company information, from working for competitors after the end of their employment.

Organizations should work with legal counsel to determine the best preventive measures for their company.

Q: What is a corporate alumni association?

Colleges and universities have long-recognized the value of maintaining relationships with their alumni. Similarly, a corporate alumni association facilitates an employer's maintaining ongoing relationships with its former employees, a.k.a. alumni.

As the labor market tightens, many employers are finding that they must be more creative in their recruitment efforts. Considering the average cost of turnover and cost per hire, connections with former employees can offer a competitive advantage by providing a pool of prequalified candidates, candidate referrals, and new business connections.

Tapping into an alumni network can also open doors to new business opportunities. Former employees find new jobs or form their own enterprises, and when they are looking for business partners, they often turn to previous employers. A company's alumni can serve as a resource for industry trends and keeping up with what competitors are doing. In addition, well-informed alumni can be powerful ambassadors for a company in the business community.

The most common means for employers to keep in touch with their alumni are through online communities and newsletters. In some cases, former employees form their own online association as an avenue for networking.

Online alumni associations can be established and maintained through independent websites such as Google, Yahoo!, and Facebook. If a comprehensive effort to maintain an alumni association is not an option, employers might consider providing their alumni with an electronic newsletter, either their standard company/employee newsletter or one geared specifically to former employees. The benefits of online publications include instant feedback from readers, interactivity, speed, savings of distribution costs, flexibility, and customization.

In addition to current job openings, alumni websites and news-letters might provide information on outplacement assistance, a directory of former alumni, alumni news, and opportunities to network and keep up with company developments. A corporate alumni association or newsletter provides former employees with networking opportunities and an avenue to continue to "work for" the company long after they are removed from the payroll—a classic win-win endeavor.

Q: Why is it important to recruit from diverse sources?

Employers should work against unlawful discrimination in hiring not only because it is the right thing to do ethically, morally, and legally, but also because discrimination can cost the employer in many ways, such as litigation, loss of quality contributors, limited expansion and innovation, and damaged reputation.

The obvious cost of discrimination is in litigation. Even if an employer wins a case in which it is accused of unlawful discrimina-tion, it must pay for court costs, not to mention the cost of the time spent in court defending the allegations. This is time that could have been spent more productively. It would be less expensive sim-ply to engage in fair recruiting practices and minimize the risk of discrimination claims.

Another cost of discrimination is the exclusion of quality contributors. If an employer does not use the broadest recruiting net possible, the employer limits itself to a candidate pool that could exclude some of the best contributors, while its competitors may be recruiting the best talent for themselves. For example, by excluding historically black colleges and universities from a list of campuses from which a company recruits, it could miss recruit-ing an Oprah Winfrey or an Ed Bradley to its journalistic ranks, a Thurgood Marshall to its law school or firm, or a Jerry Rice to its football team. Simply put, discrimination in hiring can cost an employer the best employees. Worse, the competitor could be getting them. It is better to cast a broad net to attract the best available employees from many sources rather than from a few.

In addition, diverse applicants could contribute to the innovation and thought leadership within an organization. New markets and greater shares of markets are often seized when intellectual, advertising, and marketing contributions come from employees with different backgrounds, not to mention the synergy created when minds that do not think alike are allowed to collaborate. For example, as the Hispanic population in this country grows, so do new markets into which a company could expand. Excluding personnel who can relate to the culture of many people in this group can reduce the company's competitiveness and viability in an increasingly Hispanic marketplace. Why miss out on the opportunity? Companies can make more headway into growing markets using a diverse group of employees.

Finally, organizations should consider the cost of a good reputation. Employers that discriminate based on race, color, religion, sex, national origin, age, disability, pregnancy, or other protected classes risk compromising their reputation for fairness. When a certain group is excluded, word will likely get out and negatively affect the company's reputation.

Q: How can a company make the best use of career fairs?

Career fairs are a great opportunity to distribute information on the company and to make a good impression on candidates.

However, without preparation and planning, career fairs can be a disappointment for recruiters. Recruiters should start the planning process for career fairs by doing research on the sponsoring organization(s) to make sure that it will attract viable and qualified candidates for the company. Employers should also consider the price for the career fair and what is included in the package to ensure that the sponsoring organization(s) will have enough media coverage to attract talent.

Next, recruiters can develop a relationship with the sponsors of the career fair, making sure that their company uses every resource made available by the sponsor, such as advertising, meet-and-greets with attendees, pre-fair invitations sent to a target audience, sponsoring raffle giveaways, and onsite interviews. The idea is to get more visibility with qualified candidates.

Finally, employers will want to prepare for the actual day of the career fair by doing the following:

- Making sure that they have enough representatives attending the career fair. Most sponsors will suggest at least two to four representatives attend, depending on the size of the company.
- Picking representatives who are knowledgeable, active, respectful, and energetic. The more interactive the representatives, the more interest the attendees will show in the company.
- Encouraging the representatives to bring contact information such as business cards. Most individuals who attend a career fair want to know that they can follow up with a specific person(s).
- Bringing applications and handouts detailing the company history, benefits information, and job descriptions.
- Arriving early to set up the table. It makes a better impression if recruiters are ready to speak with attendees when they stop at the booth.
- Staying until the end of the career fair. Sometimes qualified applicants are unable to get time off to attend the beginning of career fairs. By staying until the end, employers will achieve maximum exposure to all candidates.
- Advertising "active positions." Attendees become frustrated

when companies are not actually recruiting for open positions at career fairs.

- Being willing to accept resumes and applications onsite, as long as such a procedure fits into the company's process. Candidates might become discouraged when told only to complete an online application.

The key to being successful at a career fair is to be visible, so employers should plan ahead.

Q: Where can I access employers that have had successful experiences hiring people with disabilities?

Comprehensive information for employers about recruiting and hiring qualified applicants with disabilities is available in the "Recruitment and Retention" section of the U.S. Department of Labor's Office of Disability Employment Policy (ODEP) website.[3]

Other employment service providers and programs include the following:

- The Employer Assistance Referral Network (EARN), a service for employers sponsored by the ODEP, helps employers find qualified applicants with disabilities. Employers may contact EARN via its website[4] or by calling 1-866-EARN NOW (1-866-327-6669).
- Vocational rehabilitation agencies.[5]
- CareerOneStop centers.[6]
- The Workforce Recruitment Program.[7]

Ways to recruit workers with disabilities include the following:

- Posting open positions at job service or workforce employment centers.
- Contacting college and university career centers.
- Partnering with disability-related advocacy organizations.

- Including people with disabilities in diversity recruitment goals.
- Posting open positions or hosting tables/booths at disability-related job fairs.
- Establishing summer internship and mentoring programs.
- Posting open positions at independent living centers.
- Using social media.

The U.S. Business Leadership Network (BLN) is the national business organization currently representing BLN chapters in 32 states and more than 5,000 employers using a "business-to-business" strategy to promote the business imperative of including people with disabilities in the workforce.[8] The BLNs provide an opportunity for employers to identify and share best practices on the employment of people with disabilities. The ODEP endorses the BLN concept of business-to-business mentoring to help create job opportunities for people with disabilities.

Other sources for information about successful employment practices are committees, councils, or commissions on employment of people with disabilities in each state. Contact information for each state is located in the "State Liaisons"[9] section of the ODEP website.

Q: What is an employee referral program?

An employee referral program is a recruiting strategy in which current employees are rewarded for referring qualified candidates for employment. Employee referral programs are popular due to lower overall recruiting costs and a high return on investment. A successful employee referral program can also lead to higher employee satisfaction and retention rates.

Most employers have a delivery system in place that communicates the open positions and the type of reward available for referring a candidate for those positions. Many programs require the applicant be hired and work for the company a specified amount of time before the reward will be paid out to the referring employee. The reward is often monetary, but it could be in nonmonetary form such as an extra day off with pay or a gift card. Some companies vary the amount of reward depending on the job level. For example, if an employee refers a staff employee, the employee might receive a different reward from an employee who refers a management-level employee. Some programs may prohibit managers from receiving a referral for positions in which they have hiring authority, or prohibit HR personnel involved in any recruitment or hiring decisions from receiving a referral.

Q: Do employee referral programs negatively affect diversity in the workplace? If so, what should HR professionals do to address the problem?

Employee referral programs are typically an effective and convenient method of recruitment for employers. The process is a cost-effective measure that can be used to tap into a large qualified talent pool and can yield higher employee satisfaction and retention rates. Candidates obtained through an employee referral program are usually good cultural fits and may need less organizational integration when hired. But though an employee referral program is a great recruiting tool, the program may create an unintentional disparate impact on some protected groups if employees refer candidates of the same race, religion, national origin, or any other protected class.

In enforcing Title VII of the Civil Rights Act, the Equal Employment Opportunity Commission prohibits employers from using neutral employment policies and practices that have a disproportionately negative effect on applicants or employees of a particular race, color, age, religion, sex (including pregnancy), national origin, or disability. Therefore, relying heavily on employee referrals as a recruitment method may jeopardize workforce diversity efforts by unintentionally creating an imbalance in the diverse makeup of the workforce—an imbalance that could continue to multiply over time. To reduce the potential for disparate impact, employers should conduct an annual analysis to measure the effect of their employee referral programs on the applicant pool, final candidates, annual hires, and the subsequent workforce population.

To avoid unintentional discrimination when managing an employee referral program, the HR department might consider implementing the following practices:

- Ensuring the company uses various recruiting mediums when advertising vacancies in the organization. This practice allows for the inclusion of various racial and ethnic groups, creating a more diverse candidate pool and workforce.
- Making certain employee referral programs are open to the entire organization and not limited to specific groups of employees, departments, or even divisions.
- Evaluating all applicants, including employee referrals, using the same qualification criteria.
- Considering setting annual limits for employee referrals. For example, limits based on the number of referrals each employee may make and on the amount of incentive pay an employee may receive for a referral can help regulate an organization's referral program.
- Conducting ongoing analyses of the workforce and the applicant pool to ensure the program remains effective and yields intended results. HR staff can analyze the diversity categories as well as the quality of hire, resulting tenure from referrals, and other factors. If the employee referral program is not having an impact and is negatively affecting the diversity of the workforce, then the program may need to be reevaluated.

- Determining where recruitment funds are best spent on an annual basis. Should recruitment funds be used for promoting and funding the employee referral program, developing internal candidates, or making more robust external recruiting efforts? Employers may want to consider shifting funds to more diverse recruiting methods when the referral program produces a negative impact.

Chapter 13

Temporary Employees, Independent Contractors, and Interns

Q: How long can a temporary employee retain temporary status before we have to consider the employee regular?

The classification of temporary employee is defined by the employer. As such, the employer has the right to determine what length of time the employee has to work to fall into a category other than temporary.

There are, however, a few things to consider when determining an employee's classification:

- Temps often count toward the number of employees considered when determining whether an employer is covered by certain laws. For example, employers should count temporary workers to determine whether a company meets the 50-employee threshold for Family and Medical Leave Act coverage if there is a continuing employment relationship, a U.S. Department of Labor opinion letter explains.[1]

- Although employers may discriminate in the administration of fringe benefits on the basis of job classifications (for example, exempt, nonexempt, temporary, regular, full time, and part time), discriminating on any other level may be unnecessarily risky. Employees doing similar jobs should be treated similarly with regard to their benefits to avoid claims of unlawful discrimination.

- Even employees classified as temporary can participate in an employer's pension plans after completing 1,000 hours of service within a 12-month period.

Hiring temps through an agency may be a better idea than hiring temps directly, but is by no means a cure-all, as federal and state laws can supersede the terms of agency-client contracts.

Employers should have clear policies on the status of temporary employees, setting specific time limits for temporary assignments. If employees in temporary classifications are denied eligibility for benefits and temporary jobs are allowed to continue without clear limits, it can be argued that the employer is denying benefits to otherwise eligible employees.

Q: What guidance exists for employers when managing the relationship with an independent contractor?

The Internal Revenue Service has rules that can provide employers with guidance on the treatment of independent contractors (ICs).[2] These rules determine the employer's degree of control and the independence of ICs and consist of the following three criteria:

- Behavioral control. An IC generally solely determines when, where, and how to work. The IC should not only determine what apparatus is needed for an assignment but have his or her own tools, including computer, workspace, and administrative support. Additional staff needed to work on an assignment should be determined, hired, and paid by the contractor. Organizations should avoid providing work schedules to contractors and requiring contractors to adhere to company policies.

  Organizations should refrain from providing training for a contractor on methods of work. This includes participation in an organization's orientation program, mandatory training programs, or any employee award and recognition programs.

- Financial control. The IC should complete a Form W-9 and provide a Taxpayer Identification Number (TIN) and Certification. A TIN can be either a Social Security number or an employer identification number. ICs are not paid through an organization's payroll and are not subject to Fair Labor Standards Act (FLSA) minimum wage and overtime pay requirements. They are usually paid a flat fee for the job at stages or intervals of the project or on completion of the project.

  The opportunity to make a profit or loss is an important factor in demonstrating financial control for an IC. ICs should generally have unreimbursed expenses for tools and equipment used on a project given that they are considered a "business," and businesses are expected to pay their own expenses. Expenses that the organization pays should be included in a written agreement or contract as a part of the cost of the entire job. ICs should not be restricted to work solely for an organization. They should be able to work for other employers while under a contract with one organization.

- Type of relationship. ICs should not complete an employment application. It is important to have a written agreement in place that specifies the nature and duration of the project and that outlines the expectations of the project and the outcome on completing the assignment.

ICs generally are not provided with benefits such as pension plans, disability insurance, paid vacation, holiday pay, sick days, or any other employee-related incentive pay. Employers should require documentation demonstrating an IC relationship, such as business or professional licenses and insurance certificates. ICs should also have their own business cards, letterhead, and contact information unrelated to the organization.

Q: What is a statutory employee?

Most employers are aware of the two most common types of relationships with an employer: an employee relationship and an independent contractor (IC)[3] relationship. In reality, the Internal Revenue
Service defines four different types of relationships: the employee,
the statutory employee, the statutory nonemployee, and the IC. To
better understand one of the least commonly known types, consider
the statutory employee as somewhere between or a mix of the IC
and employee type of relationship.

A statutory employee is an IC; however, the worker is to be
treated as an employee by statute (by law) for certain employment
tax withholdings. In a true IC situation, an employer is not permitted to withhold any taxes as this would jeopardize the IC relationship and create an employee relationship. However, in certain
professions designated by the IRS, the person still operates as an
IC under common law rules, but certain taxes must be withheld—
thereby creating a middle-ground type of relationship called a statutory employee.

Under the IRS guidelines for meeting the requirements of statutory employee, the employer is instructed to withhold Federal Insurance Contributions Act (FICA) taxes on the employee's income.
Because statutory employees pay FICA tax through their employer,
they are not liable for self-employment tax; however, they must still
report their wages, income, and allowable expenses.

The IRS provides guidelines for statutory employees, including
designated categories and three required conditions required for
withholding Social Security and Medicare taxes.

Q: Can interns be independent contractors?

Internships focus on providing on-the-job training and experience
to individuals who have an educational background in a particular
field of study, allowing them to apply their learning in a real-world

setting for future career growth and development. Independent Contractors (ICs) are individuals who are self-employed and do not require supervision or direction in completing an assignment or project. The employer controls only the direction of the results. ICs[4] are responsible for filing their own federal and state tax requirements and for providing their own equipment and tools to complete the project. ICs usually offer their services to the general public and are people who are in an independent trade, business, or profession.

Interns receive guidance and direction from the employer, including daily job duties, training, and coaching. Services performed by an intern are most likely controlled by the employer, and once an employee-employer relationship exists, an intern cannot be classified as an IC.

Unpaid interns would not be employees or ICs; rather, they would be considered "trainees" and comparable to volunteers.

Q: Can an independent contractor or consultant manage company employees?

Allowing independent contractors (ICs)[5] or consultants to manage company employees is not for frugal or risk-adverse employers and is generally not a recommended practice. Ics or consultants are often hired for their specialized expertise. The intention is that the relationship will be short-term and focused on providing services that existing organizational employees are unable to provide. Furthermore, ICs and consultants are usually engaged using consulting agreements or contracts, which outline the services they will provide, the manner and means for providing these services, and the expected results.

Consultants and ICs are bound by the terms of their consulting agreement or contract, not by the organization's personnel policies, employee handbook, or employment-at-will doctrine.

Managing employees, on the other hand, typically involves

overseeing and enforcing the organization's personnel policies and procedures. Educating and coaching employees on how to adhere to the company's personnel policies and procedures, culture, and values through orientation and other types of training is usually a management responsibility. These are just a few examples of the "behavioral control" and "relationship of the parties" criteria that are often used to distinguish an employee from an independent contractor. Both the Internal Revenue Service and the U.S. Department of Labor (DOL) may refer to these criteria when evaluating whether a worker has been properly classified as an independent contractor. The consequences for misclassification can be extremely costly to the organization. Managers can be long-term or newly hired employees. Although they are hired with the expectation that their employment will be long term, they may be hired under the employment-at-will doctrine or an employment contract. As employees, they are subject to federal, state, and local employment laws and their employer's policies. In addition to their responsibilities for managing employees and enforcing the company's personnel policies and procedures, some managers may be responsible for managing company functions that, according to guidance from the DOL, "are an integral part of the employer's business," including supervision of the company's employees. Permitting ICs or consultants to manage company employees blurs the lines used to distinguish whether a worker is an employee or an IC.

This confusion can be costly to employers, especially if they fail to withhold and pay Social Security, Medicare, and unemployment taxes, and fail to withhold income taxes. Federal and state wage and hour enforcement may also have been compromised, along with effective and meaningful employee relations.

Chapter 14
Terminations and Downsizing

Q: How often should exit interview results be presented to senior managers? What should be reported?

Although there is no rule of thumb on how frequently results of exit interviews should be presented to senior managers, it should merit inclusion on their agenda at least quarterly. Doing so less frequently consigns this information to a "nice to have" but not critical data category. This is especially true following economic downturns when executives have a tendency to allow low turnover to foster complacency—and the suspicion that employees have no place to go to duplicate their pay and benefits. Therefore, senior managers need a pulse check on this metric at least quarterly.

In terms of what to report, management needs to be aware of what it is doing right and where it may be off track. HR leaders should organize raw exit data into meaningful categories that indicate areas to sustain and areas to remedy in order to decrease voluntary terminations. The following are sample reporting categories that are broad enough to classify any employee departure:

- Management. Unsatisfactory management or supervisory interactions with staff.
- Competitive practices. Less-than-favorable working conditions, pay, benefits, or recognition incentives when compared with competitors.
- Career potential. Lack of career path, job growth, or development plans.

- Work/life balance. Lifestyle issues, hours of work, and family commitments.

The report on employees' reasons for leaving can then serve as management's call to action for controlling the exits as well as enhancing the company's ability to meet employee expectations and to retain talent.

Thus, the role of HR leaders in the exit interview process is multipurpose. First, they solicit exit comments. Second, they organize data and present it to senior managers. Finally, they use this information to maintain practices that work and develop plans to reengage staff and cure dissatisfaction, resulting in increased retention.

Q: What criteria should be used in selecting employees for layoff?

In a perfect world, such decisions could be eradicated by ranking all jobs within the organization into specific job categories and by eliminating the positions no longer necessary to the continued success of business operations. Unfortunately, this is not a perfect world, and carrying out widespread layoffs can pose greater challenges and risks to employers. Several options are available when planning dreaded, but sometimes necessary, workforce reductions. Employers should carefully plan layoff selection before executing an organizational downsizing to ensure that selection criteria do not result in disparate treatment or have an adverse impact on protected groups. In addition, companies should research the federal Equal Employment Opportunity Commission and the state fair employment practice laws to minimize inherent risks of potential discriminatory charges.

Although it is virtually impossible for any employer to truly obtain risk-free status in implementing workforce reductions, carefully planned and executed downsizing plans used in conjunction with good documentation and layoff policies (which have been reviewed by legal counsel) can be an employer's strongest defense against allegations of discrimination. Employers in unionized environments need to take additional precautions to ensure that an existing collective bargaining agreement is not violated.

Selection for Downsizing

Seniority-Based Selection

With seniority-based selection, the "last-hired/first-fired" concept is used. Because seniority-based systems reward employees for their tenure, there is a lower risk that older workers will sue employers for age discrimination under the Age Discrimination in Employment Act (ADEA). However, using seniority does not protect the employer from further risks for potential discrimination against other protected groups.

Employee Status-Based Selection

Employers who have part-time or contingent workers on their payrolls may want to lay off those workers first to ensure greater job security for remaining core workers. Unless an employer's workforce is made up largely of contingent workers, this method alone may not be sufficient to meet downsizing needs, and it may need to be used in conjunction with other selection criteria.

Merit-Based Selection

Although this method of selection is often a preferred choice among many managers because of its added flexibility for weeding out marginal or poorly performing employees, it should be scrutinized carefully. Because merit selection criteria are based either in part or in whole on performance evaluation information (which is not always objective and may contain rater biases), this method has not been proven to provide an accurate qualitative means for ranking the differences among individual employees' performance in selecting employees for layoff.

Skills-Based Selection

With this type of system, employers can sometimes retain those workers who have the most sought-after skills. However, this method may cause a company to retain younger workers with needed and versatile skill sets, and to lay off older workers who may not have the necessary skills. The older workers are protected from discrimination by the ADEA.

Multiple Criteria Ranking

Although all of the above methods can be equally effective when planned carefully, perhaps the most effective method of selection is using a combination of all the criteria previously discussed. Below is a sample of the ranking criteria used by some organizations that have implemented selection policies based on multiple criteria such as seniority, skill, and performance considerations:

- Employee's promotability and attitude.
- Employee's knowledge, skills, abilities, and versatility.
- Employee's education and experience levels.
- Employee's quantity and quality of work.
- Employee's attendance history.
- Employee's tenure within the company.

Q: What are "bumping" rights?

Bumping usually occurs during a reduction in force in a union or civil-service setting and results when a more senior employee's job is eliminated, and instead of that employee losing employment, he or she "bumps" a less senior employee and takes that employee's job.

For example, a production manager with bumping rights whose job was cut due to budgeting can take an assembler job of a less senior employee, and the assembler would lose his job—unless, of course, he also has bumping rights and would "take" the job of another less senior employee, resulting in a domino effect.

Bumping rights are usually negotiated in union contracts but are not required by the National Labor Relations Board.

Salary and benefits for the employee's new position may be adjusted to match the pay grade or range for that position. Some employers offer an alternative to bumping if an employee chooses not to exercise his or her rights, such as a layoff recall list, which is used to notify employees of future vacancies. Employees who choose not to exercise their rights to bump may be disqualified from unemployment benefits as a result because they are ultimately refusing an offer of work.

Q: What is the difference between a furlough, a layoff, and a reduction in force?

All three of these terms describe actions intended to achieve cost savings by reducing a company's payroll costs. Even though the words have been used interchangeably, their true meanings are quite different.

A furlough is considered to be an alternative to layoff. When an employer furloughs its employees, it requires them to work fewer hours or to take a certain amount of unpaid time off. For example, an employer may furlough its employees one day a week for the remainder of the year and pay them for only 32 hours instead of their normal 40 hours each week. Another method of furlough is to require all employees to take a week or two without pay sometime during the year.

An employer may require all employees to go on furlough, or it may exempt some employees who provide essential services. Generally, though, the theory is to have the majority of employees share some hardship as opposed to a few employees' losing their jobs completely. Employers must be careful when furloughing exempt employees, so that they continue to pay the employees on a salary basis and do not jeopardize their exempt status under the Fair Labor Standards Act (FLSA). A furlough that encompasses a full work-week is one way to accomplish this, because the FLSA states that exempt employees do not have to be paid for any week in which they perform no work.

A layoff is a temporary separation from payroll. Employees are laid off because there is not enough work for them to perform; their employer, however, believes that this condition will change and intends to recall the employees when work again becomes available. Employees generally are able to collect unemployment benefits while laid off without pay, and frequently an employer will allow them to maintain benefits coverage as an incentive to remain available for recall.

Once management has determined that an employee will not be recalled to work, the layoff becomes permanent and is more accurately called a reduction in force, or a termination. A reduction in force involves a permanent cut in head count that can also be accomplished by means of attrition. Some employers use layoff as a euphemism for what is actually a permanent separation. This may be confusing to affected employees, allowing them to believe that recall is a possibility, thus preventing them from devoting their full energies toward locating a new position.

Q: Can we include employees who have performance problems in a reduction in force?

Yes, employers may include employees with performance problems in a reduction in force (RIF) if the employer has solid written documentation of the business purpose for the RIF, as well as defendable reasons for how and why employees were chosen for layoff.

After a company has determined that a RIF is the best way to meet its financial goals, a business analysis should be conducted to determine the employees who will be affected. Nondiscriminatory employee selection criteria should be developed and used to select the employees who will be laid off.

Performance criteria may be used, and employers may consider previous performance reviews and other performance documentation, such as warnings or any type of disciplinary actions. Employers may also wish to use seniority as a determining factor.

However, a RIF is based on a business need to cut costs or to better align resources, so the business is able to meet overall goals and objectives—and it is not the best way to manage performance issues. Laying off employees with performance problems, who are in necessary positions, may create problems for the company. The employer will need to fill the positions, a situation that could lead to claims of wrongful discharge or discrimination.

Using a RIF to manage performance can also lead to morale problems with staff who remain employed. Employees often can see when their peers have performance problems. When strong-performing employees find out that poor-performing employees received severance payments, and management did not address the performance issues, it can lead to decreased respect toward managers, as well as waning employer loyalty and increased turnover.

Q: Can an employer terminate and rehire an employee as an independent contractor doing the same job?

For someone to work as an independent contractor (IC) for an organization, he or she must meet certain classification requirements by both the Internal Revenue Service (IRS)[1] and the U.S. Department of Labor (DOL)[2] that serve to show that the individual is clearly working for himself or herself and not the employer. If the person will continue to perform the same work in the same capacity as an employee, then, most likely, he or she will not qualify as an IC.

If an employee quits to launch a business that uses its own resources and supplies and serves additional clients, it may be possible to contract that person to do some work, but it would not be on a full-time basis, and the company would have limited control because that person is no longer the company's employee.

On the other hand, if the change is simply to allow the employer to avoid employment costs, such as benefits and tax expenses, and the employer intends to maintain the same level of control and provide full-time work, equipment, and supplies, the worker would unlikely meet the definition of an IC.

It is inaccurate to assume that an employee may be terminated and hired as an IC. Both the IRS and the DOL have increased their audits on contractor and employee classifications, so employers should review federal regulations before taking such an action, as well as seek legal counsel.

Q: How long after eliminating a position should we wait before filling a position?

Although no laws dictate a specific time frame to wait after a layoff before filling a position, there are several reasons an employer should proceed cautiously when filling a position that was recently part of a reduction in force or job elimination. Handled improperly, an employer may be accused of using the position elimination as a pretext for what would otherwise be an unlawful termination. A former employee may attempt to sue an employer for wrongful discharge within state and federal statute of limitations time frames.

As with all negative employment actions, the reasons should be lawful and justifiable. If there truly is no longer a need for a position, and the employer can show business need for the elimination, it would generally be permissible to terminate employment for position elimination. It would be reasonable for an outsider to then believe this to be a permanent elimination, and not expect the employer to rehire for the position within a short time frame.

However, the legitimacy of the position elimination may be in doubt if the employer does try to rehire for the position within six months or less, for example, and the former employee finds out the new hire or replacement is younger than himself or herself (age 40 or under); of a different race, religion, or gender; or is less qualified. If the employer cannot show the business need for the elimination, it may find itself in legal trouble. In short, employers should not attempt to use position elimination as a quick fix for a subpar employee, even in stressful economic times.

What about general layoffs and recalls? Again, there are no laws that require an employer to recall laid-off employees unless it has a policy or union contract stating otherwise. In general terms, a layoff indicates that an employer does not have enough work to keep everyone on staff but that it may expect to have more work at some point in the future.

Although the law does not require employers to recall laid-off employees or show them preference, there is nothing stopping them from applying for rehire when jobs are reposted. Former employee-applicants should be given the same consideration as all other candidates, barring any rehire policies the employer may have.

Does this mean then that employers should always use layoff and not position elimination as the reason for termination? No. HR professionals should guide their organization in truthful terminations for both legal and ethical reasons. It is important for HR professionals to follow their normal progressive discipline process for performance issues, to educate managers on unlawful discrimination concerns, and to stop potentially unlawful terminations before they occur.

Chapter 15
Veterans

Q: What is the difference between the VETS 100 and VETS 100A report forms, and what types of organizations should file each?

Federal government contractors and subcontractors that have contracts of a certain dollar amount must file either one or both of these forms each year by September 30. Prior to 2002, the Vietnam Era Veterans' Readjustment Assistance Act (VEVRAA) required federal contractors and subcontractors with contracts worth $25,000 or more to annually collect certain categories of data on the covered veterans in their workforce and to report these data on the Federal Contractor Veterans' Employment Report VETS-100 (VETS-100 Report) form.[1] The Jobs for Veterans Act (JVA) amended VEVRAA's reporting requirements by both contract dollar amount and veteran categories and tasked the U.S. Department of Labor (DOL) with promulgating regulations to implement these amendments.

In May 2008, the VETS department of the DOL issued regulations that created the new requirements for the VETS-100A Report form to be used starting September 30, 2009, for all contracts entered into or modified after December 1, 2003, of $100,000 or more.[2] The JVA amendments do not relieve contractors and subcontractors of their VETS-100 reporting requirements since 2002, nor do they relieve them of such requirements going forward. If a federal contractor or subcontractor still has a contract entered into or modified prior to December 1, 2003, of $25,000 or more, it must continue to file the VETS-100 form annually on its entire workforce. Additionally, if a federal contractor or subcontractor has contracts entered into or modified after December 1, 2003, of $100,000 or more, it must file the VETS-100A form annually, on its entire workforce. If a federal contractor or subcontractor has contracts that meet each of these requirements, it must file both the VETS-100 and the VETS-100A Report forms annually on its entire workforce. The regulations make it clear that one report will not suffice, as the veteran categories have changed, and some veterans might not be reported if only one report form were filed. In the event that a contract entered into prior to December 1, 2003, of $25,000 or more was modified after December 1, 2003, then the new requirements would apply, and if over $100,000, only the VETS-100A Report form would need to be filed.

The covered veteran categories for the VETS-100 form are as follows:

- Special disabled veterans.
- Vietnam-era veterans.
- Recently separated veterans.
- Other protected veterans.

The covered veteran categories for the VETS-100A form are as follows:

- Disabled veterans.
- Other protected veterans.
- Recently separated veterans.
- Armed Forces Service Medal veterans.

Q: What is veterans' preference, and is it required in the private sector?

Veterans' preference is a method government agencies use to give eligible veterans preference over other applicants. However, veterans' preference does not guarantee veterans a job, nor does it apply to internal actions such as promotions and transfers.

Veterans' preference can be confusing. Veterans' preference eligibility is based on a number of factors such as dates of active duty service, receipt of a campaign badge or a Purple Heart, or a service-connected disability.[3] Not all active duty service members may qualify for veterans' preference. Only veterans discharged or released from active duty in the armed forces under honorable conditions are eligible for veterans' preference.

Veterans' preference is not required in the private sector, although some states, such as Washington, have enacted such legislation.

The U.S. Department of Labor's Veterans' Preference Advisor[4] provides additional information on veterans' preference hiring in the federal government, as does the U.S. government's Feds Hire Vets page.[5]

Chapter 16

Visas and I-9 Compliance

Q: Can a company refuse to consider a candidate who is not eligible to work in the United States and would require sponsorship for an H-1B visa?

An employer is not required by law to sponsor an H-1B visa for a candidate who is ineligible to work in the United States. An employer may have a policy, applicable to all positions, that it does not sponsor employment visas. Or an employer may have a policy listing specific positions (typically hard-to-fill positions) that are eligible for sponsorship.

Before an employer decides whether to sponsor an employee for work authorization, the employer should look at its staffing plan. Some employers, due to the nature of the services they provide, tend to have hard-to-fill positions, whereas others find that they are able to meet their staffing requirements fairly easily. For companies part of the latter group, sponsorship might not be a feasible recruiting tool.

Because sponsorship of an employee's work authorization takes time and requires an often ongoing financial investment, an employer should consider the process and responsibilities involved. With the sponsorship of an H-1B visa, the job must be for a what the U.S. Citizenship and Immigration Services deems a "specialty occupation," and an employer needs to file a Labor Condition Application to start the process.[1] An employer must also adhere to certain stipulations regarding wages and working conditions. Further, an employer will be required to pay for certain costs associated with work-related visas it decides to sponsor—in particular, the labor certification.

Although an employer is not required to sponsor an employee, it may do so. However, an employer must act consistently with the company sponsorship policy to avoid discrimination issues. Employers are encouraged to discuss sponsorship with an immigration attorney before proceeding.

Q: How do I hire a foreign national to work in the United States?

Due to labor shortages in particular areas, employers may need to hire foreign labor to place people in hard-to-fill positions. Examples where foreign labor is used include certain "specialty occupations" as defined by the U.S. Citizenship and Immigration Services (USCIS) such as information technology or finance or seasonal positions such as in the agricultural field, ski resorts, or amusement parks.

Under certain conditions, U.S. immigration law may allow a U.S. employer to file a Form I-129 (Petition for a Nonimmigrant Worker) with the USCIS to hire foreign labor.[2] Upon approval of the petition, the prospective employee may then apply for admission to the United States or for a change of nonimmigrant status if he or she is already in the United States.

In most situations, for employment-based nonimmigrant visa categories, the employer starts the process by filing Form I-129 with the USCIS. However, there are some cases in which the employer must file a certification with the U.S. Department of Labor (DOL) before filing Form I-129. These certification forms attest, for example, a need for labor or a difficulty in finding candidates for jobs that may be filled by foreign laborers.

The DOL requires that employers file a Labor Condition Application (LCA)[3] or Application for Alien Employment Certification[4] and/or a consultation report from labor organizations before filing a petition (Form I-129) with the USCIS. Certification from the DOL is required only for the H-1B, H-1C, H-2A, and H-2B non-immigrant classifications. The forms required are the following:

- For H-1B nonimmigrants, an LCA.
- For H-1C nonimmigrants, an attestation.
- For H-2A and H-2B nonimmigrants, an Application for Temporary Employment Certification.[5]

The employer must file in accordance with DOL instructions. Once DOL certifications (if necessary) and the petition (Form I-129) are complete, the prospective employee's visa category must meet the occupational requirements covered under the petition. There is a multitude of nonimmigrant, employment-based visa categories. The USCIS provides a list with occupational requirements.[6]

The USCIS also provides guidance on related issues such as filing one petition for more than one employee—called a blanket petition—as well as information on expediting a petition or extending/changing nonimmigrant status. See the USCIS Employer Guide for key information and related forms.[7]

Employers new to this process or in doubt about any forms or visa requirements are recommended to consult legal counsel to ensure the correct process is followed and required documents are filed.

Q: What is an H-1B visa?

An employer seeking to employ a foreign worker temporarily in a specialty occupation uses the H-1B visa program. Specialty occupations require theoretical and practical application of a body of highly specialized knowledge along with at least a bachelor's degree or its equivalent. Examples include architecture, engineering, mathematics, physical sciences, medicine and health, education, and business specialties, among others. H-1B is also used for fashion models of distinguished merit and ability.

The H-1B visa classification requires a sponsoring U.S. employer. The employer must file a labor condition application (Form ETA 9035) with the U.S. Department of Labor.[8] The application contains declarations, including payment of prevailing wages for the position and working conditions offered. The employer must then file an I-129 petition with the U.S. Citizenship and Immigration Services (USCIS) and, unless specifically exempted under law, pay filing fees.[9] Based on USCIS petition approval, the foreign worker may apply for the H-1B visa, admission, or a change of nonimmigrant status.

Q: What must an employer do to obtain an H-1B visa for a potential employee?

The visa application process usually takes several months. To sponsor an employee through the H-1B visa, an employer usually needs to submit only two forms: the Labor Condition Application (LCA)[10] and the Petition for Nonimmigrant Worker.[11]

The first form is the LCA, Form ETA-9035, also called a labor attestation.[12] In this form, the employer must attest to the following items that are intended to ensure that U.S. workers are not displaced:

- The employer offers the "proper wage" for the position and has documentation of what the prevailing wage is for the job in question. Employers will need to prepare a "prevailing wage study" to make this attestation.
- The employer will provide working conditions that will not adversely affect the working conditions of similarly situated U.S. workers.
- The employer must certify that there is no strike or lockout where the nonimmigrant will work.

- The employer has notified the employees through the bargaining representative for unionized employees, or, in a nonunionized environment, the employer must physically post in two conspicuous locations for 10 consecutive days a notice of the filing in the classification for which the H-1B nonimmigrant is sought.

The LCA is filed with the U.S. Department of Labor.

Second, on approval of the LCA, the employer must file a Petition for Nonimmigrant Worker, Form I-129 (along with $110 filing fee), with the U.S. Citizenship and Immigration Services service center that has jurisdiction over the area where the nonimmigrant will work or train. For most employers, a $1,000 filing fee must be submitted with the form. Exempt organizations, such as higher education institutes or affiliated nonprofit entities, need not submit this fee. However, petitioners seeking exemption from the fee must complete Part B of the form.

Q: How should an employer transfer a candidate's H-1B visa from his or her current employer?

H-1B visas are nonimmigrant visas for persons to work in the United States in specialty occupations. A specialty occupation requires theoretical and practical application of a body of knowledge along with at least a bachelor's degree or its equivalent.

Commonly, H-1B visas are requested by companies for highly skilled information technology workers. However, the visas are also requested for positions in many other fields, such as engineering, mathematics, medicine, law, and the arts.

If an employer finds a candidate who is already working in the United States on an H-1B visa, the employer can transfer the candidate's visa from his or her current employer. U.S. Citizenship and Immigration Services must be notified of any changes in employment status through Form I-129 (H-1B petition).[13] This form can be filed electronically.

Employers should be aware that to file the petition for transfer of the nonimmigrant, the following conditions must be met:

- The nonimmigrant must have lawfully entered the United States.
- The petition must be for new employment and must be filed before the end of the nonimmigrant's period of authorized stay.
- The nonimmigrant must not have been employed without authorization since his or her lawful admission to the United States and before the filing of the petition.

There are fees associated with an H-1B transfer. An employer filing the I-129 form must pay a petition fee as well as additional fees unless exempt under Part B of the H-1B Data Collection and Filing Fee Exemption Supplement or covered by the Fraud Prevention and Detection Fee under the H-1B Visa Reform Act.

The American Competitiveness in the Twenty-First Century Act provides that nonimmigrant workers with H-1B status may begin working for a new employer once the new H-1B petition has been filed. This means that the I-129 has to be only filed and not approved. Approval or denial will be sent at a later date. There is a greater probability of approval if the nonimmigrant is working in the same capacity in the new job as in his or her previous job. If the petition is ultimately denied, the employer will have to make the necessary adjustment at that time.

Q: What is an H-2B certification?

The H-2B nonimmigrant program permits employers to hire foreign workers to come temporarily to the U.S. and perform temporary nonagricultural services or labor on a one-time, seasonal, peak-load, or intermittent basis. The H-2B visa classification requires the U.S. Secretary of Homeland Security to consult with appropriate agencies before admitting H-2B nonimmigrants. The U.S. Department of Homeland Security (DHS) regulations require that, except for Guam, the petitioning employer must first apply for a temporary labor certification from the U.S. Secretary of Labor indicating that (a) there are not sufficient U.S. workers who are capable of performing the temporary services or labor at the time of filing the petition for H-2B classification and at the place where the foreign worker is to perform the work, and (b) the employment of the foreign worker will not adversely affect the wages and working conditions of similarly employed U.S. workers. The U.S. Department of Labor (DOL) will review and process all H-2B applications on a first-in, first-out basis.

Employers seeking to employ temporary H-2B workers must file an Application for Temporary Employment Certification,[14] Appendix B.1,[15] and their recruitment reports to the Chicago National Processing Center (NPC). When filing an application with the Chicago NPC, the employer does not need to name each temporary foreign worker it wishes to employ. An employer may submit a request for multiple unnamed foreign workers as long as each worker is to perform the same services or labor, on the same terms and conditions, in the same occupation, in the same area of intended employment, during the same period of employment. Certification is issued to the employer, not to the worker, and is not transferable from one employer to another or from one worker to another.

The applicant must be a U.S. employer with a job opportunity located within the United States. The job opportunity must be temporary. A job opportunity is considered temporary under the H-2B classification if the employer's need for the duties to be performed is temporary, regardless of whether the underlying job is permanent or temporary. It is the nature of the employer's need, not the nature of the duties, that is controlling. Except where the employer's need is based on a one-time occurrence, the Secretary of Labor will, absent extenuating circumstances, deny an Application for Temporary Employment Certification when the employer has a recurring seasonal or peak-load need lasting longer than 10 months.

Part-time employment does not qualify as employment for temporary labor certification under the H-2B program. Only full-time employment can be certified.

Q: How can an employer file an Application for Permanent Employment Certification, ETA Form 9089?

The employer has the option of filing an application electronically (using online forms and instructions) or by mail. However, the U.S. Department of Labor (DOL) recommends that employers file electronically. Not only is electronic filing by its nature faster, but filing electronically provides prompts that assist in the completion of the ETA Form 9089.[16]

An application for a Schedule A occupation must be filed by mail with the appropriate U.S. Department of Homeland Security (DHS) office and not with a DOL National Processing Center.

The customer-friendly ETA Foreign Labor Certification website[17] allows employers to register and establish an account and then electronically complete and submit an Application for Permanent Employment Certification, ETA Form 9089.

The website also allows employers that frequently file permanent employment certification applications to set up secure files within the ETA electronic filing system with information common to any application the employer files. Under this option, each time an employer files an ETA Form 9089, the information common to all its applications (for example, employer name and address) will be entered automatically, and the employer will need to enter only the data specific to the application at hand.

Q: What is the foreign labor certification process for hiring foreign workers?

Hiring foreign workers for employment in the U.S. normally requires approval from several government agencies. In most instances, employers first seek labor certification from the U.S. Department of Labor. Once the application is certified (approved) by DOL, the employer must petition the U.S Citizenship and Immigration Services for a visa. Approval of a labor certificate does not guarantee a visa issuance. The Department of State will issue an immigrant visa number to the foreign worker for U.S. entry. Applicants must also establish that they are admissible to the U.S. under the provisions of the Immigration and Nationality Act.

The foreign labor certification process is the responsibility of the employer, not the employee; however, the employee can benefit from understanding these programs. The actual procedures depend on the nature of the visa being requested: permanent, H-1B, H-2A, H-2B, or D-1.

Q What is a permanent labor certification?

A permanent labor certification issued by the U.S. Department of Labor (DOL) allows an employer to hire a foreign worker to work permanently in the United States. In most instances, before the U.S. employer can submit an immigration petition to the Department of Homeland Security's U.S. Citizenship and Immigration Services (USCIS), the employer must obtain an approved labor certification request from the DOL's Employment and Training Administration (ETA). The DOL must certify to the USCIS that there are no qualified U.S. workers able, willing, qualified, and available to accept the job at the prevailing wage for that occupation in the area of intended employment and that employment of the alien will not adversely affect the wages and working conditions of similarly employed U.S. workers.

As of March 2005, ETA Form 750 applications were no longer accepted under the regulation in effect prior to March 28, 2005, and instead new ETA Form 9089[18] applications had to be filed under the labor certification for the Permanent Employment of Aliens in the United States (PERM)[19] at the appropriate national processing center. Applications filed under the regulation in effect prior to March 28, 2005, have continued to be processed at the appropriate backlog elimination center under the rule in effect at the time of filing. Only if an employer chose to withdraw an earlier application and refile the application for the identical job opportunity under the refile provisions of PERM, was a previously filed ETA Form 750 application filing date considered under the PERM regulation.

The DOL processes applications for permanent employment certification, ETA Form 9089. The date the labor certification application is filed is known as the filing date and is used by USCIS and the U.S. Department of State (DOS) as the priority date. After the LCA is approved by the DOL, it should be submitted to the USCIS service center with a Form I-140, Immigrant Petition for Alien Worker.[20] The DOS Visa Bulletin announces the priority dates currently being processed.[21]

The qualifying criteria for a permanent labor certification are the following:

- Applications filed on or after March 28, 2005, must file using the new PERM process and adhere to the new PERM regulations.
- The employer must hire the foreign worker as a full-time employee.
- There must be a bona fide job opening available to U.S. workers.

Job requirements must adhere to what is customarily required for the occupation in the U.S. and may not be tailored to the foreign worker's qualifications. In addition, the employer should document that the job opportunity has been and is being described without unduly restrictive job requirements, unless adequately documented as arising from business necessity.

The employer must pay at least the prevailing wage for the occupation in the area of intended employment.

Q: How does an employer go about sponsoring a worker for a green card?

An alien worker who wants to obtain lawful permanent U.S. residency but does not have a relative in the United States who could serve as his or her sponsor may seek the employer's sponsorship.

First, it must be determined if the individual meets the criteria for any of the U.S. Citizenship and Immigration Services' (USCIS) five occupation-based categories for permanent residency. The following descriptions are drawn from the USCIS website that details the requirements and procedures.

- Priority workers. These are foreign nationals who possess extraordinary abilities in the arts, sciences, education, athletics, or business; who are outstanding professors or researchers; or who are managers or executives subject to international transfer to the United States.
- Aliens of exceptional ability. These foreign nationals possess exceptional abilities in the sciences, arts, or business; are professionals with advanced degrees; or are physicians who will practice medicine in a medically underserved area of the United States.
- Skilled and other workers. Professionals with basic degrees are in this category, as are skilled workers. Positions in the skilled-workers category, according to the USCIS, are

not seasonal or temporary and require at least two years of experience or training. The training requirement may be met through relevant post-secondary education. Workers in positions requiring less than two years of vocational training are considered "other workers" and generally are subject to quotas and longer waiting periods.

- Special immigrants. These include foreign national religious workers and foreign nationals who are current or former U.S. government employees abroad.
- Immigrant investors. Among these individuals are those who invest $1 million in an active U.S. business enterprise employing at least 10 U.S. workers for two years. Also eligible are those who have invested or are in the process of investing at least $500,000 in a "targeted employment area, which is an area that has experienced unemployment of at least 150 percent of the national average rate or a rural area as designated by the U.S. Office of Management and Budget."[22]

Presuming the foreign national meets the criteria of one of the above categories, the employer in most instances submits a labor certification request—Form ETA 750—for the applicant to the U.S. Department of Labor's (DOL) Employment and Training Administration, which then grants or denies the request.[23]

A labor certification is a statement from the DOL that a position at a particular company is "open" because no U.S. workers who are qualified for the job are available.

Such certification is generally required for an alien to be admitted as a permanent resident, but it is not required for priority workers or for physicians agreeing to work in areas certified by the U.S. Department of Health and Human Services as medically underserved.

In the next step, the employer files an immigrant visa petition—Form I-140, Petition for Alien Worker.[24] The form requires information about the alien to support the claim of the alien's occupation-based category. The employer acts as the sponsor for the applicant. Then the U.S. Department of State gives the applicant a number to indicate an immigrant visa has been assigned to the applicant.

An applicant who is already in the United States must apply to adjust to permanent resident status after a visa number becomes available.

Form I-140 must be filed at the USCIS Service Center that serves the area where the immigrant will work. Detailed information is provided in the instructions for Form I-140. Filing requirements differ for each of the five categories.

For details on eligibility of foreign nationals, the application process, and related matters, visit the USCIS website. Employers that are considering sponsoring a foreign national for permanent residency and that wish to file a petition on their behalf should consult with an immigration attorney to obtain a full understanding of what is involved in the process and what the implications of sponsorship may be for them.

Q: What is an employer's responsibility when an employee with an H-1B visa is terminated?

H-1B visas are nonimmigrant visas that allow foreign workers in specialized occupations to reside and work in the United States for a limited time period. To qualify, a foreign worker must be sponsored by a U.S. employer. Employers can terminate an H-1B visa worker without penalty; however, doing so causes the employee to immediately lose status to live and work in the United States. Because a termination has immediate consequences for the employee, it triggers obligations for the employer.

When terminating, the employer must begin by providing clear, unequivocal notification of a "bona-fide termination" to the employee. It must be done in writing and clearly indicate that the employment relationship has been terminated.

Employers are required to notify the U.S. Citizenship and Immigration Services (USCIS) by letter when there has been any "material change" to the terms and conditions of an approved H-1B petition, such as when the employment of an H-1B employee has been terminated. Recommended procedure includes a certified letter to the USCIS Service Center that approved the H-1B, providing the date of termination and a request to revoke the H-1B petition. Employers should immediately notify the USCIS to limit any claims for unpaid wages for the period after the employee's termination until the end of the contract. In addition, employers should inform the antifraud section of the U.S. consulate in which the visa stamp was originally issued that the H-1B petition has been withdrawn. Finally, the employer must notify the U.S. Department of Labor (DOL) that it is withdrawing the labor condition application (LCA).[25]

Due to the employee's immediate loss of status to remain in the United States, the employer has an obligation to provide "reasonable costs of transportation" for the employee back to his or her last place of residence. The obligation does not extend to family members or for personal items such as furniture and belongings. (If the employee voluntarily terminates employment, the employer is not obligated to provide the cost of return transportation.) The employer can offer either a direct purchase of a plane ticket or cash payment. However, an employer cannot force an employee to accept the ticket. If the employee refuses to accept a ticket or cash payment for a ticket, the employer should request that the employee sign a statement, with independent witnesses if possible, indicating that the employee declines acceptance of the ticket or cash.

Employers may want to explore other options before terminating, out of compassion for the employee. An H-1B worker can legally transfer his or her visa to another employer before being terminated or before the visa expires. Provided there is enough notice, an employer wishing to terminate an H-1B employee could give that worker reasonable time to find a new petitioning employer; however, there is no requirement to do so. Another option is a practice known as "benching," in which the employer may temporarily lay off the employee or place the employee on a leave of absence or temporary status before terminating. Doing so may give the employee enough time to find another employer without immediately losing his or her status in the United States. In these instances, the USCIS requires the terms and conditions of employment described in the work visa petition to be maintained, including paying the employee his or her normal wages despite being temporarily laid off or placed on leave—frequently making this option not affordable to the employer.

The employer should document all steps it has taken to comply with immigration law. If there is a layoff or furlough, an employer may have compensatory obligations under the LCA. In addition, there are risks of being sued under state contract law if, for example, offer letters and other writings constitute an implied contract. There are risks of discrimination claims if H-1B employees are not treated as other similar employees in such situations. Employers need to be mindful of the special requirements affecting H-1B workers to avoid additional liability. Employers are advised to consult with legal counsel on issues involving H-1B workers.

Q: How does NAFTA affect hiring employees from Canada and Mexico?

The North American Free Trade Agreement (NAFTA) allows for a relatively easy process for qualified professional citizens of Canada and Mexico to obtain a nonimmigrant visa, called a TN visa, to work in the United States for an initial period of up to three years.

The benefits of a TN visa are that it typically costs less and takes less time for approval than many other types of visas. Companies that hire under NAFTA must ensure the applicant is a citizen of either Canada or Mexico and will be working in one of the jobs listed in the NAFTA Professional Job List.[26] The person must also possess the qualifications of the profession as listed in the minimum educational requirements and alternative credentials. Companies must also ensure that the position available in the United States requires a NAFTA professional and is temporary, without the intent to establish permanent residence; the applicant must work for a U.S. employer and have required documentation. Full- or part-time employment is acceptable, but self-employment is not permitted. Categories of professionals that are eligible to seek admission as TN nonimmigrants include accountants, engineers, lawyers, pharmacists, scientists, and teachers.

The requirements for citizens of Canada and Mexico differ. Canadian citizens usually do not need an actual visa as a NAFTA professional, although a visa can be issued to qualified TN visa applicants on request. A Canadian citizen without a TN visa can simply take the required documentation to the port of entry and, if approved, be awarded "TN status" to enter and work in the United States. Mexican citizens are required to obtain a TN visa to request admission to the United States, and an interview at the U.S. embassy or consulate is required before arriving at the port of entry.

To obtain a TN visa, the applicant must submit Form DS-160, the Online Nonimmigrant Visa Electronic Application.[27] Applicants must also have a valid passport for U.S. travel, a photograph in the required format, and a letter from the U.S. employer indicating the following:

- Language stating that the position requires the employment of a person in a professional capacity, consistent with the NAFTA Chapter 16, Annex 1603, Appendix 1603.d.1.[28]

- The activity in which the applicant will be engaged and the purpose of entry.
- Anticipated length of stay.
- Educational qualifications or appropriate credentials demonstrating professional status.
- Evidence of compliance with U.S. Department of Homeland Security regulations and state laws.
- Arrangements for pay.

In addition, the applicant's employer must submit proof that the applicant meets the minimum educational requirements or has the alternative credentials set forth in the NAFTA agreement, along with the documentation proving the applicant's work experience.

When followed properly, NAFTA can be a means to open an additional candidate pool for hard-to-fill positions.

Q: How can an employer prevent the employment of illegal workers?

There are several ways an employer can prevent the employment of illegal workers.

The first is consistent, careful completion of I-9 forms[29] for all new hires, reverification when an employee's eligibility to work in the United States is expiring, and routine auditing[30] of the employer's I-9 forms.

Diligent initial completion and reverification of I-9 forms may not always ensure that employees are legally working due to the prevalence of counterfeit documents and stolen identities. To assist employers in verifying employment eligibility and preventing employment of illegal workers, the federal government offers free, voluntary programs.

One program in which employers may voluntarily participate is the Social Security Number Verification Service, offered by the Social Security Administration (SSA).[31] Once an employee submits a Social Security number for I-9 documentation or for payroll tax withholding, an employer may contact the SSA to verify that the number is a valid one and that it matches the name the employee is using. If the employer finds a mismatch, it would direct the employee to resolve the discrepancy within a reasonable period to continue to be employed.

Another program is the E-Verify Program,[32] run jointly by the U.S. Citizenship and Immigration Services (USCIS) and the U.S. Department of Homeland Security (DHS). E-Verify involves verification checks of both the SSA and DHS databases using an automated system to verify the employment authorization of all newly hired employees. This program allows participating employers to confirm employment eligibility of all newly hired employees, improves the accuracy of wage and tax reporting, and protects jobs for authorized U.S. workers.

The most recent program is the Immigration and Customs Enforcement (ICE) Mutual Agreement between Government and Employers Program (IMAGE).[33] IMAGE seeks to accomplish greater industry compliance and corporate due diligence through enhanced federal training and education of employers. Companies that comply with the terms of IMAGE will become IMAGE certified.

As a first step in becoming IMAGE certified, employers must agree to a Form I-9 audit by ICE. They must also use the E-Verify program when hiring employees and adhere to a series of best practices. These include the creation of internal training programs for completing employment verification forms and detecting fraudulent documents.

IMAGE partners must also arrange for audits by neutral parties and establish protocols for responding to letters received from federal and state government agencies indicating that there is a discrepancy between the agency's information and the information provided by the employer or employee. ICE also asks employers to establish a tip line for employees to report violations and mechanisms for companies to self-report violations to ICE.

Chapter 17
Workforce Planning and Readiness

Q: How does trend analysis fit into workforce planning?

By definition, workforce planning is the strategic alignment of an organization's human capital with its business direction. It is important for an organization to develop a strategic workforce planning process that will identify the human capital needs required to meet business objectives. Typically, workforce planning is a five-step process:

1. Set the strategic direction.
2. Analyze the workforce.
3. Develop an action plan.
4. Implement the action plan.
5. Monitor, evaluate, and revise the plan.

Assuming, then, that the organization has already completed step 1 of the process—setting strategic direction—the second logical step is to conduct a workforce analysis. The workforce analysis phase of the planning model has several components:

- Supply analysis, which identifies the competencies of the organization, analyzes the demographics of the staff, and recognizes trends such as turnover.
- Demand analysis, which measures future activities and workloads.
- Gap analysis, which compares information from the supply analysis and demand analysis to identify the gaps between the current organizational competencies and those needed in the future workforce.

- Solution analysis, which involves developing strategies for closing the competency gaps and reducing surplus competencies.

The trend analysis is an essential element of the supply analysis phase. Whereas the competency analysis provides baseline data on the existing organization and present staff, the trend analysis provides data describing how trends such as turnover will affect the workforce and is a key element in the overall planning process.

Trend data, though, are not limited to turnover data. They may also include the following:

- Hiring and retirement patterns.
- Years of service.
- New-hire retention rate.
- Transfers.
- Promotions.

Trend information can help predict the supply of skills that may be available in the future and project the future workforce supply needed. Using the example of turnover rates, the following questions illustrate how an analysis of these data can be used to model or predict future workforce staffing needs:

- Are there certain groups with increasing worker turnover?
- What are the factors affecting turnover? Can they be identified?
- Has turnover reduced the skill set of a certain group?

Careful planning and a thorough analysis of data can help the workforce planner build a strategic plan for addressing the future needs of the organization.

Q: How should a company develop a staffing plan?

Staff planning is a systematic process to ensure that an organization has the right number of people with the right skills to fulfill business needs. Employers must take into account internal and external changes and must integrate HR planning with the company's business plan. The following list describes the various steps needed to develop a staff planning program:

- Job description. The HR department first develops a job description with input from the hiring manager.

- Job requirements. Next, human resources and the manager create a detailed and useful set of job requirements. This information can help HR staff determine whether qualified candidates already exist or whether they can be developed within the company before recruiting externally. Some of the questions to ask are (a) what skills, knowledge, and abilities are required for the job; (b) what are some of the characteristics of the people who succeed or fail in the job; (c) what qualifications are needed for the job; and (d) how does the job relate to others.

- Fair employment considerations. To avoid illegal screening of applicants with disabilities, the HR department should list job duties describing only what the necessary tasks are, not how the tasks are normally performed.

- Assessment of current employees' skills. This step involves gathering skills information from employees to help find qualified internal candidates before recruiting from outside.

- Turnover trends. Documenting turnover trends can help predict how many people will leave the organization. This information will prepare for peak recruitment times.

- Business trends. HR professionals should consider two issues when analyzing business trends: the internal changes and the external factors; both will affect staff planning. Internal adjustments include changes in work shifts, workforce demographics, and downsizing. External factors include mergers or acquisitions and legislation.

Once all relevant information has been collected, the HR department can forecast its staffing and recruitment needs.

Q: How do I conduct a job analysis to ensure the job description actually matches the duties performed by the employee in the job?

Job descriptions are used for a variety of reasons. They are a tool for recruiting, determining salary ranges and levels or grades, establishing job titles, creating employee's job goals and objectives, and conducting performance reviews. They can also be used for career planning, creating reasonable accommodations, and meeting legal requirements for compliance purposes. Given their multiple uses, written job descriptions should accurately reflect the employees' current job duties and responsibilities.

Employers should audit their job descriptions every few years, usually in conjunction with a compensation study and whenever the organization's purpose, mission, or structure changes. One way to audit or create job descriptions is to conduct a job analysis. Job analysis is the process of gathering, examining, and interpreting data about the job's tasks and responsibilities. It generally includes tracking an employee's duties and the duration of each task; observing the employee performing his or her job; interviewing the employee, managers, and others who interact with the employee; and comparing the job to other jobs in the same department and job grade or job family. An important concept in job analysis is that it is an evaluation of the job, not of the person doing the job. The final product from a job analysis includes a thorough understanding of the essential functions of the job; a list of all duties and responsibilities; a percentage of time spent for each group of tasks; the job's relative importance in comparison with other jobs; the knowledge, skills, and abilities needed to perform the job; and the conditions under which the work is completed.

There are many ways to perform a job analysis, but all require the cooperation of the employee in the position, his or her manager(s), and others the employee works closely with while performing his or her job duties. The HR department can involve employees in the process by having them complete job analysis forms.

The following activities will help human resources provide the best analysis of a particular job:

- Interviewing employees, asking them specific questions about their job duties and responsibilities.
- Obtaining log sheets from employees with information about each of their tasks and the time spent on each task for at least one full workweek.
- Completing desk audits where HR professionals observe employees doing their jobs at different times of the day and days of the week, and tracking what they do and for how long.
- Interviewing supervisors and managers and other employees, clients, and customers the employee may interact with while performing the job.
- Comparing the job to other jobs in the department as well as to the job grade or job family to show where it falls on the pay scale.

If more than one person is doing the same job, human resources should observe and obtain feedback and information from each person. Finally, the HR department should review its findings with the employees who do the job as well as with their supervisors and managers to tweak the findings until human resources has an accurate reflection of the job duties and responsibilities.

Q: How should a downsized organization approach staffing needs?

Following periods of economic turbulence, downsized organizations need to rethink their approach to building their capabilities instead of simply implementing the staffing strategies used in the past. An employer needs to analyze its workforce composition to determine how best to respond to improvements in terms of its business sustainability and its flexibility in meeting growth opportunities.

First, the employer should develop metrics to identify its staffing needs in terms of core staff (internal employees performing core business processes) versus contingent staff and determine what is optimal for the organization's business maintenance and development. The best approach to this determination is not through benchmarks or best practices but through a focus on internal workload processes, task balancing and leveling, and creating productivity metrics to build staffing requirements from the bottom up rather than from the top down.

Before hiring new staff, the organization must address internal questions on whether to require part-timers to increase hours and days of work, to liberalize the use of overtime (consistent with organizational health and safety concerns), or to expand the use of weekend and shift work periods to avoid logistical issues that can cause an employer to increase facilities size and expenses. Once these questions are answered and priorities are established, the employer can use decision trees for recalling staff, re-staff in the event recalls are no longer viable, or handle increasing work volume through other arrangements.

A company may no longer be able to staff its enterprises with only internal staff and remain competitive; thus, the employer should consider new ways of looking at workforce composition to better meet organizational needs.

Staffing managers must take the lead in determining how to effectively and efficiently meet both core and contingent staffing needs by identifying, analyzing, and proposing cost-effective workplace planning strategies that facilitate the organization's sustainability in the future. A 21st-century workforce planning perspective is one that understands the value associated with all facets of workplace planning, including outsourcing, back office operations, rural sourcing, offshoring, professional employer organizations, staffing firms, and independent contractors.

Q: I would like to partner with local colleges to develop a workforce with the skills that our company needs. How can I get started?

To be successful at partnering with a local college, an employer must be willing to devote time, energy, and resources. The more the students know about the company, the more interested the students will be in the company. Employers that are innovative with creating visibility on college campuses are often more successful at finding individuals with desired skill sets.

An employer should start the partnering process by focusing on the schools that closely fit the needs of its business. For instance, an engineering company may want to focus on schools with strong engineering programs. Companies can contact the school or college career services department to schedule a time to talk with staff about recruiting on campus.

When meeting with the career services representative, HR professionals should ask about the programs in place for employers to use. They can discuss their company goals with the representative and try to determine the best way to achieve those goals. Inquiring about the success stories of other employers on that campus may also be helpful. HR professionals should be willing to explore opportunities outside of the traditional career fair, for example, internships, co-op programs, presentations at student club meetings, scholarships for students, class presentations, school events sponsorship, and workshops on resume writing and interviewing techniques. An employer must find innovative ways for the students to see that the company is really interested in them and why they would want to work for the company.

Once the opportunities for outreach on campus have been explored, the HR department can decide which outreach efforts will give the employer the most visibility. Next, HR staff can devise a plan and timetable and discuss it with the school or college career services representative. Once an employer has set up a plan of action, the employer must commit to it. Students want to see execution and follow-up. After each semester or school year, the HR department should evaluate the outreach efforts and be willing to revamp the plan as needed. The employer needs a consistent plan for maintaining contact with the school and students. Again, visibility is key.

In summary, developing a partnership with local colleges will take time, energy, resources, and creativity. Exploring all opportunities to increase the company's visibility will allow the students to see what the company has to offer and will also allow the company to see what the students have to offer.

Chapter 18
Working Conditions

Q: Can employers change an employee's job duties, schedule, or work location without his or her consent or prior notification?

Yes, in most cases employers may make these changes without the employee's consent. Generally, unless an employment contract or a collective bargaining agreement states otherwise, an employer may change an employee's job duties, schedule, or work location without the employee's consent. In terms of notifications, none are required by law unless the schedule is changed upon the employee's arrival to work, and the employee's total hours of work that day have been reduced from what was known to be scheduled the prior day. In that case, some states have what are known as "reporting pay" or "show up pay" regulations that may require a minimum amount of hours to be paid to employees who have experienced a loss of hours that day. Check the state-by-state On Call/Call Back/Reporting Pay chart on the Society for Human Resource Management's website for specific state guidance.[1]

If an employee is on Family and Medical Leave Act (FMLA) leave, the employer's right to make changes is limited. The act protects an employee's job duties, schedules, and work location by prohibiting changes that include the following:

- Changing the essential functions of the job to preclude the taking of leave.
- Reducing hours available to work to avoid employee eligibility.
- Transferring the employee to an alternative position to dis-

courage the employee from taking leave.
- Otherwise placing a hardship on the employee.

Upon returning from FMLA leave, employees must be reinstated to their job or an equivalent one. An equivalent position is one that is virtually identical to the employee's former position in terms of pay, benefits, and working conditions, including privileges, perquisites, and status. It must involve the same or substantially similar duties and responsibilities, which must entail substantially equivalent skill, effort, responsibility, and authority. The employee is ordinarily entitled to return to the same shift, or to a similar or equivalent work schedule. FMLA does not prohibit an employer from accommodating an employee's request to be restored to a different shift, schedule, position, or location that better suits the employee's personal needs upon return from leave, or from offering a promotion to a better position. However, an employee cannot be induced by the employer to accept a different position against the employee's wishes.

In addition, schedule and duty changes made in retaliation for employees' exercising their employment rights—such as filing a workers' compensation claim, taking FMLA leave, filing a wage or discrimination claim, or whistle-blowing—would violate the employee protections within those laws. And certainly, changes made based on unlawful discrimination (for example, only women have their hours cut or authority reduced) would be unlawful.

Q: What factors should employers consider prior to instituting a telecommuting policy?

Telecommuting is a flexible work arrangement that allows employees to work at home, on the road, or from another satellite location for all or, more commonly, part of their workweek. There are business considerations when deciding to allow an employee to work from home. Questions to consider include the following:

- Is there executive and top-level management support?
- Can the budget be made available to cover expenses?
- Will the company's technology support the arrangement, so the employee experiences a seamless workflow?
- Is the position conducive to telecommuting (for example, a receptionist cannot do his or her job properly by telecommuting)?
- Will the arrangement be offered to all employees or just employees in certain positions? Will the offered arrangement be the same for all employees?
- Will a certain number of days per week or every day be allowed?
- Will there be a minimum performance level that must be maintained by telecommuters?
- Will there be a minimum length of service for eligibility?
- How will performance and work output be monitored?
- How will working hours be monitored?
- How will the manager communicate with telecommuters?
- Does the employee have the technology systems and skills needed to be successful as a telecommuter?
- How will technology systems that are not working be handled (for example, must employees come into office)?
- How will telecommuting employees participate in meetings?

Most successful telecommuting programs include the following elements:

- An application from employees who meet the policy criteria for telecommuting and wish to become a telecommuter.
- Frequent contact between the manager and the employee. This should be a combination of informal contact as well as

scheduled regular check-in meetings and may consist of progress reports required weekly or even daily.

- The employee's willingness and ability to have appropriate, regular contact with the main office on a formal and social basis.
- Comparable participation in office events, performance evaluation, and promotion opportunities.
- Clear articulation that telecommuting is not a substitute for child care and an expectation that the employee will have appropriate child care arrangements when working from home.
- A requirement that telecommuters spend at least some time on a regular basis working at the office.
- Training for nontelecommuters on how to work with telecommuters and the benefits to the organization of doing so (for example, improved team-building skills).
- A telecommuting agreement between the employer and the employee with clear expectations. The agreement could initially be on a trial basis for a set period of time, with the option for renewal and a clause stating that either party may end the agreement at any time. Items to be covered in the agreement include the following:
  » Work hours.
  » Amount and form of communication with the office.
  » Number of days per week telecommuting versus working in the office, as well as specific days for each.
  » Equipment and supplies to be provided by the company.
  » Reimbursable expenses and reimbursement procedure.
  » Workspace setup, including ergonomics.
  » Safety issues and responsibility for injuries.
- Annual (or more frequent, if necessary) review and update of telecommuting agreements.

Additional issues to consider include the following:

- Information asset security. Who has responsibility for maintaining hardware and software, and how will the maintenance be performed?
- Workers' compensation. What is the scope of liability under state law?
- Insurance. Does the employer need special protection to insure telecommuters?
- Tax and zoning issues. There may be local ordinances limiting the type of business that can be conducted from an employee's home. It is the employee's responsibility to check with state and local agencies.
- Unions. Telecommuting is a condition of work and must be vetted by the union.

Q: What are some common types of alternative schedules?

Common types of alternative schedules include the following:

- Part-time. Part-time workers regularly work less than a full-time schedule. Part-time schedules may include working only a few days a week or working fewer hours five days a week.
- Flextime. Flextime occurs when employers have an expectation that employees work a standard amount of hours during a week or day, but the employers allow flexibility in employees' starting and ending times. Some employees, due to family or personal obligations or preferences, work early in the morning and leave earlier in the afternoon. Other flextime employees may prefer or need to start later in the day and work into the evening.
- Compressed workweeks. These allow employees to work a standard number of work hours over less than a five-day period in one week or a 10-day period in two weeks. The most common compressed workweek schedule is probably

4/10s (10 hours a day for four days a week). Many employers allow exempt employees to work 9/9s biweekly. This means the employee regularly works 9 hours a day with one day off every other week. The 9/9 schedule is usually not preferable for nonexempt workers due to the concern of overtime pay every other week. Additionally, in the summertime some employers often close early on Fridays, and therefore employees are scheduled to work nine-hour days Monday through Thursday and only a half-day on Friday.

- Telecommuting. Telecommuting allows employees to perform work from a remote location (usually a home office) rather than commute to the company facility. Employers commonly offer telecommuting on a part-time or periodic basis (for example, one or two days a week or month). Due to ongoing technological advances, this practice will likely increase as more and more jobs can be performed completely remotely.
- Job sharing. This is the practice of two different employees' performing the tasks of one full-time position. A full-time position filled by two employees who have complementary part-time work schedules can ensure coverage during normal work hours.

Q: What are some job and employee characteristics that make a good fit for telecommuting?

Successful telecommuting arrangements are based on job characteristics, employee characteristics, and manager characteristics.

Jobs best suited for telecommuting are those with the following characteristics:

- They require independent work.
- They need little face-to-face interaction.
- They require concentration.
- They result in a specific, measurable work product.

- They can be monitored by the output, not by the time spent doing the job.

Employees best suited for telecommuting arrangements are those with the following characteristics:
- They can work productively on their own.
- They are self-motivated and flexible.
- They are knowledgeable about their job.
- They have a low need for social interaction.
- They are dependable and trustworthy.
- They have an above-average performance record.
- They are organized.
- They have good communication skills.

Managers who work most effectively with telecommuters are those with the following characteristics:
- They empower and trust their employees.
- They learn how to manage by results or output rather than by time spent working.
- The encourage feedback and communication.
- They are effective problem-solvers or facilitators.
- They support telecommuting as a concept and work to make arrangements successful.
- They effectively plan and organize their work and the work of subordinates to achieve results.

Q: What are some potential benefits and risks of tele-commuting, both for the employer and employee?
Telecommuting can have great benefits for both the employer and the employee; however, there can be risks as well.

The following are among the potential benefits an employer may enjoy when it allows workers to telecommute:

- Savings on office space.
- Improved employee morale.
- Increased productivity.
- The ability to meet community clean air objectives.
- The ability to hire individuals who would otherwise be unable or unwilling to work (for example, people with disabilities or parents with young children who wish to work unusual hours to accommodate child care needs).
- A decrease in absenteeism and turnover.

Benefits enjoyed by telecommuters include the following:
- Increased flexibility in balancing work and home needs.
- Greater ability to concentrate on work, leading to increased productivity.
- Improved morale and productivity.
- Savings in work-related expenses (for example, commuting, clothing, meals).
- Reduced stress due to an easier commute, increased control over work hours, and other factors.

For employers, the potential drawbacks associated with telecommuting include:
- Inability to directly supervise telecommuters.
- Costs of establishing an appropriate work environment.
- Liability and implementation issues.
- Resentment of telecommuters by nontelecommuters.
- Lack of face-to-face communication and inaccessibility during normal business hours.

For telecommuters, the possible drawbacks include the following:
- Less social interaction.
- Greater need to be self-motivated and focused on work over

distractions of home.

- Added responsibility of setting up and maintaining the workspace.
- Tendency to work longer hours.

Q: What is hoteling?

Hoteling is an approach to help reduce the cost of office space accommodations, and it can be a resourceful method for workplace utilization. Basically, hoteling involves rotational use of office space when there are employee absences.

By analyzing employee absence data, employers can determine a percentage of space that is generally available from day to day. Employee absences can vary due to travel, vacation, or leaves of absence or if employees work temporarily at a client site. Thus, hoteling can provide an effective alternative to ineffective office space use.

To determine whether hoteling is viable, management must first assess internal work patterns through a comparative analysis to calculate the number of employees who are out of the office. Once that number has been determined, decisions must be made about what space is available and when it can be used. The employer would then need to set up a system for employees to reserve space and equipment. Employees can book workstations and reserve appropriate network access and communication equipment.

Q: What should employers consider when instituting a compressed workweek?

A compressed workweek has its advantages. It can save employees one round trip to work each week, adding up to significant savings. Even before gas prices began to escalate, employers used compressed workweeks as an informal work/life benefit for employees with long commutes or other family obligations. Now, many employers are also choosing to take the cost savings a step further by actually closing their businesses one day each week.

This decision may benefit both the employer and employees, but employers must consider a number of factors before moving to this type of schedule.

Not all jobs are suited for a compressed workweek schedule. This is particularly true for jobs that require a set schedule to ensure proper coverage and customer interaction. HR professionals should conduct a job analysis to ensure that all tasks and responsibilities of the job can be accomplished within the compressed workweek schedule.

It is also important that HR professionals consider the dynamics between employees being left to work the traditional schedule versus those who are working the compressed schedule. If not handled properly, resentment may develop among employees unable to use the compressed workweek benefit. To help prevent perceptions of unfairness, employers must create eligibility criteria and apply the criteria consistently to all.

Paid holidays are a significant consideration when implementing a compressed schedule. Though not legally mandated, most employers provide a certain number of paid holidays to their employees. HR professionals should plan how they are going to handle these paid holidays for employees who are already working a compressed workweek schedule. Those who have a four-day workweek typically use one of three approaches to eligibility for holiday pay. Some employers pay for holidays occurring only on the employee's regularly scheduled workday. Other employers establish a "floating" holiday system whereby employees are given a certain number of days off in exchange for working on typical holidays. A third approach that employers choose is to simply provide an extra day of pay while requiring the employee to work on that holiday, essentially paying the employee "double time" for the holiday.

Endnotes

Chapter 1

1. U.S. Equal Employment Opportunity Commission, "2013 EEO-1 Survey," http://www.eeoc.gov/employers/eeo1survey/index.cfm.

2. U.S. Equal Employment Opportunity Commission, "EEO-1 Instruction Booklet," http://www.eeoc.gov/employers/eeo1survey/2007instructions.cfm.

3. U.S. Equal Employment Opportunity Commission, "EEO-1 Application," https://egov.eeoc.gov/eeo1/eeo1.jsp.

4. U.S. Equal Employment Opportunity Commission, "EEO-1 Registration," https://egov.eeoc.gov/eeo1/register.jsp.

5. U.S. Equal Employment Opportunity Commission, "2013 EEO-1 Survey."

6. U.S. Equal Employment Opportunity Commission, "EEO-1: Who Must File," http://www.eeoc.gov/employers/eeo1survey/whomustfile.cfm.

7. U.S. Department of Labor, "Determining if You Are a Federal Contractor or Subcontractor Subject to the Laws Enforced by OFCCP," http://www.dol.gov/elaws/esa/ofccp/determine.asp.

8. U.S. Government Printing Office, "Title 41. Public Contracts and Property Management. §60-2.10. General purpose and contents of affirmative action programs," last modified June 5, 2014, http://www.ecfr.gov/cgi-bin/text-idx?c=ecfr&sid=ebbf29 c1d009950ae2f520c0123b4889&rgn=div8&view=text&node =41:1.2.3.1.2.2.1.1&idno=41.

9. U.S. Department of Labor, "Executive Order 11246," http://www.dol.gov/compliance/laws/comp-eeo.htm.

10. U.S. Census Bureau, "Equal Employment Opportunity (EEO) Tabulation," http://www.census.gov/people/eeotabulation.

11. U.S. Government Printing Office, "Title 41. Public Contracts and Property Management. §60-2.14. Determining availability," last modified June 5, 2014, http://www.ecfr.gov/cgi-bin/text-idx?c=ecfr&sid=b3ebabb54dc7b768ea49568ac361d4a2&rgn=div5&view=text&node=41:1.2.3.1.2&idno=41%20-%2041:1.2.3.1.2.2.1.5#41:1.2.3.1.2.2.1.5.

12. U.S. Department of Labor, Office of Federal Contract Compliance Programs, "Small Contractor Affirmative Action Program (AAP) Job Group Availability Determinations," http://www.dol.gov/ofccp/scaap.htm.

13. U.S. Department of Labor, Office of Federal Contract Compliance Programs, "Internet Applicant Recordkeeping Rule," http://www.dol.gov/ofccp/regs/compliance/faqs/iappfaqs.htm.

Chapter 2

1. Answers.USA.gov, "Get Military Discharge Records (DD-214)," http://answers.usa.gov/system/templates/selfservice/USAGov/#!portal/1012/article/3792/Get-Military-Discharge-Records-DD-214.

2. Government Printing Office, "Title 29 C.F.R., Part 1607—Uniform Guidelines on Employee Selection Procedures," (1978), http://www.gpo.gov/fdsys/pkg/CFR-2011-title29-vol4/xml/CFR-2011-title29-vol4-part1607.xml.

3. Society for Human Resource Management, "Affirmative Action: Definition of Applicant: Does OFCCP's Recent Rule on the Definition of Internet Applicant Mean All Electronic Submissions of Interest Are Applicants?", HR Q&A, April 11, 2014, http://www.shrm.org/TemplatesTools/hrqa/Pages/CMS_014915.aspx.

4. Society for Human Resource Management, "Equal Employment Opportunity/Discrimination Laws," January 2014, http://www.shrm.org/LegalIssues/StateandLocalResources/StateandLocalStatutesandRegulations/Documents/EEO-discrimination.pdf.

5. Society for Human Resource Management, "Affirmative Action: Internal AAP Checklist," http://www.shrm.org/templatestools/samples/hrforms/pages/affirmativeactioninternalaapchecklist.aspx.

6. U.S. Equal Employment Opportunity Commission, "EEOC Issues Enforcement Guidance," news release, April 25, 2012, http://www.eeoc.gov/eeoc/newsroom/release/4-25-12.cfm.

7. Job Accommodation Network, *Technical Assistance Manual: Title I of the ADA*, 1992, http://askjan.org/links/adatam1.html.

8. U.S. Equal Employment Opportunity Commission, *How to Comply with the Americans with Disabilities Act: A Guide for Restaurants and Other Food Service Employers*, January 19, 2011, http://www.eeoc.gov/facts/restaurant_guide.html.

9. Job Accommodation Network, *Technical Assistance Manual: Title I of the ADA*, 1992.

10. Ibid.

11. Job Accommodation Network, "Employees' Practical Guide to Negotiating and Requesting Reasonable Accommodations under the Americans with Disabilities Act," http://askjan.org/Eeguide/IIRequest.htm.

12. USNEI, "Recognition of Foreign Qualifications: Professional Recognition," December 2007, http://www2.ed.gov/about/offices/list/ous/international/usnei/us/profrecog.doc.

13. U.S. Department of the Treasury, "Resource Center: Specially Designated Nationals List (SDN)," last modified May 30, 2014, http://www.treasury.gov/resource-center/sanctions/SDN-List/Pages/default.aspx.

14. U.S. Department of the Treasury, "Resource Center: When Should I Call the OFAC Hotline?", last modified December 6, 2010, http://www.treasury.gov/resource-center/faqs/Sanctions/Pages/directions.aspx.

15. U.S. Department of Labor, "Executive Order 11246," http://www.dol.gov/compliance/laws/comp-eeo.htm.

Chapter 3

1. Federal Trade Commission, "FACTA Disposal Rule Goes into Effect June 1," news release, June 1, 2005, http://www.ftc.gov/news-events/press-releases/2005/06/facta-disposal-rule-goes-effect-june-1.

2. Society for Human Resource Management, "Drug & Alcohol Testing: Must All Companies Follow the FCRA Guidelines for Drug Tests?" HR Q&A, November 12, 2012, http://www.shrm.org/TemplatesTools/hrqa/Pages/FCRAguidelinesdrugtests.aspx.

3. National Student Clearinghouse website, http://www.student-clearinghouse.org.

4. U.S. Department of Education, "The Database of Accredited Postsecondary Institutions and Programs," http://ope.ed.gov/accreditation.

5. Council for Higher Education Accreditation website, http://www.chea.org.

6. National Association of Professional Background Screeners website, http://www.napbs.com.

7. U.S. Citizenship and Immigration Services, "Frequently Asked Questions: Federal Contractors and E-Verify," http://www.uscis.gov/uscis-tags/12195/employment-verification.

Chapter 4

1. Federal Trade Commission, Bureau of Consumer Protection Business Center, "Using Consumer Reports: What Landlords Need to

Know," December 2001, http://www.business.ftc.gov/documents/bus49-using-consumer-reports-what-landlords-need-know.

2. Federal Trade Commission, "Advisory Opinion to Islinger (06-09-98)," http://www.ftc.gov/policy/advisory-opinions/advisory-opinion-islinger-06-09-98.

3. Ibid.

Chapter 6

1. Federal Register, "Department of Labor, Office of Federal Contract Compliance Programs, 41 C.F.R. Parts 60-250 and 60-300," Vol. 78, No. 185, September 24, 2013, http://www.gpo.gov/fdsys/pkg/FR-2013-09-24/pdf/2013-21227.pdf.

2. Government Printing Office, "Title 41: Public Contracts and Property Management: Part 60-300," June 2, 2014, http://www.ecfr.gov/cgi-bin/text-idx?c=ecfr&sid=3b71cb5b215c393fe9 10604d33c9fed1&rgn=div5&view=text&node= 41:1.2.3.1.9&idno=41.

3. U.S. Department of Labor, "Executive Order 11246," http://www.dol.gov/compliance/laws/comp-eeo.htm.

4. Government Printing Office, "Title 29 C.F.R., Part 1607—Uniform Guidelines on Employee Selection Procedures," (1978), http://www.gpo.gov/fdsys/pkg/CFR-2011-title29-vol4/xml/CFR-2011-title29-vol4-part1607.xml.

5. U.S. Equal Employment Opportunity Commission, "Title VII of the Civil Rights Act of 1964," http://www.eeoc.gov/laws/statutes/titlevii.cfm.

6. U.S. Equal Employment Opportunity Commission, "Questions and Answers: Religious Accommodation in the Workplace," last modified on January 31, 2011, http://www.eeoc.gov/policy/docs/qanda_religion.html.

7. Ibid.

8. Ibid.

9. *Hosanna-Tabor Evangelical Lutheran Church and School v. Equal Employment Opportunity Commission*, 565 U.S. ___ (2012), http://www.supremecourt.gov/opinions/11pdf/10-553. pdf.

Chapter 7

1. Society for Human Resource Management, "Sample Interview Questions," http://www.shrm.org/TemplatesTools/Samples/ InterviewQuestions/Pages/default.aspx.

Chapter 8

1. V. A. Graicunas, "Relationship in Organization," in *Papers on the Science of Administration*, ed. by Luther Gulick and Lyndall F. Urwick (New York: Institute of Public Administration, 1937), 183-187; Lyndall F. Urwick, "The Manager's Span of Control," *Harvard Business Review* (May-June 1956): 39-47.

Chapter 9

1. Federal Register, "Executive Order 12564—Drug-Free Federal Workplace," http://www.archives.gov/federal-register/codification/executive-order/12564.html.
2. Government Printing Office, "Title 29 C.F.R., Part 1607—Uniform Guidelines on Employee Selection Procedures (1978)," http://www.gpo.gov/fdsys/pkg/CFR-2011-title29-vol4/xml/ CFR-2011-title29-vol4-part1607.xml.
3. U.S. Department of Labor, "Executive Order 11246," http:// www.dol.gov/compliance/laws/comp-eeo.htm.

Chapter 11

1. See Richard P. Finnegan, *The Power of Stay Interviews for Engagement and Retention* (Alexandria, VA: Society for Human Resource Management, 2012).

Chapter 12

1. Society for Human Resource Management, "Recruiting: Sourcing: What Is a Corporate Alumni Association?" HR Q&A, November 27, 2012, http://www.shrm.org/Templates-Tools/hrqa/Pages/CMS_017156.aspx.

2. Society for Human Resource Management, "Glossary: E: Ethics," http://www.shrm.org/templatestools/glossaries/business-terms/pages/e.aspx.

3. U.S. Department of Labor, "Disability Employment Policy Resources by Topic: Recruitment and Retention," http://www.dol.gov/odep/topics/RecruitmentAndRetention.htm.

4. Ask EARN website, http://askearn.org.

5. Council of State Administrators of Vocational Rehabilitation website, http://www.rehabnetwork.org.

6. CareerOneStop website, http://www.servicelocator.org.

7. Workforce Recruitment Program website, https://wrp.gov.

8. U.S. Business Leadership Network website, http://www.usbln.org.

9. U.S. Department of Labor, "Disability Employment Policy Resources by Topic: Directory of State Liaisons," http://www.dol.gov/odep/contact/state.htm.

Chapter 13

1. U.S. Department of Labor, "Opinion Letter: FMLA2004-1-A," April 5, 2004, http://www.shrm.org/TemplatesTools/hrqa/Documents/2004_04_05_1A_FMLA.pdf.

2. Internal Revenue Service, "Independent Contractor Defined," April 4, 2014, http://www.irs.gov/Businesses/Small-Businesses-&-Self-Employed/Independent-Contractor-Defined.

3. Ibid.

4. Ibid.

5. Ibid.

Chapter 14

1. Internal Revenue Service, "Independent Contractor Defined," April 4, 2014, http://www.irs.gov/Businesses/Small-Businesses -&-Self-Employed/Independent-Contractor-Defined.

2. U.S. Department of Labor, "Fair Labor Standards Act Advisor: Independent Contractors," http://www.dol.gov/elaws/esa/ flsa/docs/contractors.asp.

Chapter 15

1. U.S. Department of Labor, "VETS 100/100A Federal Contractor Reporting," http://www.dol.gov/vets/vets-100.html.

2. Ibid.

3. U.S. Government Printing Office, "5 U.S.C. 2108-Veteran; Disabled Veteran; Preference Eligible," http://www.gpo.gov/ fdsys/granule/USCODE-2011-title5/USCODE-2011-title5-par-tIII-subpartA-chap21-sec2108/content-detail.html.

4. U.S. Department of Labor, "Welcome to the Veterans' Preference Advisor," http://www.dol.gov/elaws/vetspref.htm.

5. Feds Hire Vets website, http://www.fedshirevets.gov.

Chapter 16

1. U.S. Department of Labor, "Labor Condition Application for H-1B Nonimmigrants," http://www.doleta.gov/regions/reg05/ Documents/eta-9035.pdf.

2. U.S. Citizenship and Immigration Services, "I-129, Petition for a Nonimmigrant Worker," last modified June 7, 2013, http:// www.uscis.gov/i-129.

3. U.S. Department of Labor, "Labor Condition Application for H-1B Nonimmigrants."

4. U.S. Department of Labor, "DOL Form ETA 750A," http://webapps.dol.gov/libraryforms/go-us-dol-form. asp?FormNumber=1.

5. U.S. Department of Labor, "Application for Temporary Employment Certification: ETA Form 9142," http://www.foreignlaborcert.doleta.gov/pdf/OMBETAForm9142.pdf.

6. U.S. Citizenship and Immigration Services, "Temporary (Nonimmigrant) Workers," http://www.uscis.gov/working-united-states/temporary-workers/temporary-nonimmigrant-workers.

7. U.S. Citizenship and Immigration Services, "'How Do I' Guides for Employers" http://www.uscis.gov/tools/how-do-i-customer-guides/how-do-i-guides-employers/how-do-i-guides-employers.

8. U.S. Department of Labor, "Labor Condition Application for Nonimmigrant Workers: ETA Form 9035 & 9035E," http://www.foreignlaborcert.doleta.gov/pdf/ETA_Form_9035_2009_Revised.pdf.

9. U.S. Citizenship and Immigration Services, "I-129, Petition for a Nonimmigrant Worker."

10. U.S. Department of Labor, "Labor Condition Application for H-1B Nonimmigrants."

11. Ibid.

12. U.S. Department of Labor, "Foreign Labor Certification," http://www.foreignlaborcert.doleta.gov/preh1bform.cfm.

13. U.S. Citizenship and Immigration Services, "I-129, Petition for a Nonimmigrant Worker."

14. U.S. Department of Labor, "Application for Temporary Employment Certification: ETA Form 9142," http://www.foreignlaborcert.doleta.gov/pdf/OMBETAForm9142.pdf.

15. U.S. Department of Labor, "Application for Temporary Employment Certification: ETA Form 9142 — APPENDIX B.1," http://www.foreignlaborcert.doleta.gov/pdf/Form_9142_AppendixB_1_012309.pdf.

16. U.S. Department of Labor, "Application for Permanent Employment Certification: ETA Form 9089," http://www.foreignlaborcert.doleta.gov/pdf/9089form.pdf.

17. U.S. Department of Labor, ETA Foreign Labor Certification website, https://www.plc.doleta.gov/eta_start.cfm?actiontype=home&CFID=36400&CFTOKEN=67643780.

18. U.S. Department of Labor, "Application for Permanent Employment Certification: ETA Form 9089."

19. U.S. Department of Labor, Employment and Training Administration, "Permanent Labor Certification," last modified May 1, 2014, http://www.foreignlaborcert.doleta.gov/perm.cfm.

20. U.S. Citizenship and Immigration Services, "I-140, Immigrant Petition for Alien Worker," http://www.uscis.gov/i-140.

21. U.S. Department of State, "Visa Bulletin," http://travel.state.gov/content/visas/english/law-and-policy/bulletin.html.

22. U.S. Citizenship and Immigration Services, "EB-5 Immigrant Investor," last reviewed/updated: July 3, 2012, http://www.uscis.gov/working-united-states/permanent-workers/employment-based-immigration-fifth-preference-eb-5/eb-5-immigrant-investor.

23. U.S. Department of Labor, "Application for Alien Employment Certification," http://www.foreignlaborcert.doleta.gov/pdf/eta750a.pdf.

24. U.S. Citizenship and Immigration Services, "I-140, Immigrant Petition for Alien Worker."

25. U.S. Department of Labor, "Labor Condition Application for H-1B Nonimmigrants."

26. U.S. Citizenship and Immigration Services, "TN NAFTA Professionals," last reviewed/updated: June 17, 2013, http://www.uscis.gov/working-united-states/temporary-workers/tn-nafta-professionals.

27. U.S. Department of State, "DS-160, Online Nonimmigrant Visa Application," http://travel.state.gov/content/visas/english/forms/ds-160--online-nonimmigrant-visa-application.html.

28. See International Center, University of Michigan, "APPENDIX 1603.D.1 OF ANNEX 1603 OF THE NAFTA," http://www.internationalcenter.umich.edu/immig/tnvisa/tn_occupationlist.pdf.

29. U.S. Immigration and Customs Enforcement, "Form I-9," http://www.uscis.gov/sites/default/files/files/form/i-9.pdf.

30. Society for Human Resource Management, "How to Conduct an I-9 Audit," HR Q&A, http://www.shrm.org/Templates-Tools/HowtoGuides/Pages/ConductanI-9Audit.aspx.

31. Social Security Administration, "The Social Security Number Verification System," http://www.socialsecurity.gov/employer/ssnv.htm.

32. U.S. Citizenship and Immigration Services, "E-Verify," http://www.uscis.gov/e-verify.

33. U.S. Immigration and Customs Enforcement, "IMAGE," http://www.ice.gov/image.

Chapter 18

1. Society for Human Resource Management, "State Call-In/Call-Back/Reporting Pay Laws," http://www.shrm.org/Legal-Issues/StateandLocalResources/StateandLocalStatutesandRegulations/Documents/Callbackcallinreportingpay.pdf.

Index

401(k), 51, 64

A
absenteeism, 164
adverse impact, 10, 58, 59, 83, 116
affirmative action plan(s) (AAP), 19, 56, 57, 85
Age Discrimination in Employment Act (ADEA), 28, 34, 52, 117, 118
aliens of exceptional ability, 139
American Competitiveness in the Twenty-First Century Act, 134
Americans with Disabilities Act (ADA), 18, 19, 23, 24, 27, 34, 47, 52, 71, 72, 79, 80, 82
Americans with Disabilities Act Amendments Act, 71
applicant pool(s), 86, 107
Application for Alien Employment Certification, 120

Application for Temporary Employment Certification, 131, 135, 136
application(s)
    form, 17
    unsolicited, 20-1
arrest record(s), 22, 23
Association of International Credential Evaluators, Inc., 32
attendance
    history, 118
    issues, 65
    policies, 66
attestation, 131, 132
at-will, 53, 54, 113, 114

B
background check, 17, 18, 20, 23, 28-9, 30, 33, 34, 45, 46, 52, 78, 87; *see* chapter 3
benefits
    fringe, 109
    package, 51, 77

plan(s), 17, 74, 91
birth date(s), 18
buddy system, 93, 94
budget, 50, 64, 76, 77, 91, 118, 159
bumping, 118-19
Bureau of Labor Statistics, 97
business objectives, 50, 149
business sustainability, 154

C

Canada, 143-44
career fairs, 102, 103, 104
CareerOneStop centers, 104
Census Bureau, 11
Census Data Tool, 11
Chamber of Commerce, 97
citizenship, 19
COBRA, 73
cognitive disabilities, 71
collective bargaining agreements (CBAs), 56, 85
College Level Examination Program, 32
college transcript, 37
compensation philosophy, 50
competencies, 67-8, 149-50
    surplus, 150
competency analysis, 150
competency gaps, 150
competitive intelligence, 64

compressed workweeks, 161, 165
confidential, 17, 29, 82, 94, 99
consistently working, 73-4
consumer
    credit report, 23
    reporting agency, 35, 45
    reports, 35-6, 45-6
contingent offers, 82
contractors,
    federal, 6, 9, 11, 12, 20-1, 34, 41, 55, 57, 85, 125
    first-tier subcontractors, 5
    independent (ICs), 121, 155; see chapter 13
    subcontractors, 5, 9, 34, 55, 125
controlled substance, 24
conviction(s), 22-3
cost of turnover, 100
cost per hire, 100
Council for Higher Education Accreditation, 37
country of birth, 19
credential evaluation services, 31
credit
    history, 23, 38
    reporting agency, 36
    reports, 35, 45

criminal records, 23, 38, 45

criterion-related validity, 59, 83

culture, 26, 64, 76, 78, 93, 94, 102, 114

D

data management techniques, 13, 15

date of birth (DOB), 28, 29

deaf, 71

defamation, 29-30, 42

degree(s), 14, 18, 31, 36, 37, 50, 110, 131, 133, 139

demographics, 149, 151

desk audits, 153

development opportunities, 51

diploma(s), 18, 36

   mills, 36-7

disability-related advocacy organizations, 104

disability-related job fairs, 105

discharge, 10, 24, 59, 127

discrimination, 8, 9, 10, 19, 23, 26, 28, 33, 34, 51, 57, 58, 59, 60, 61, 64, 66, 86, 101, 117, 118, 121, 130, 143, 158

   age, 52, 117

   anti-, 18, 34

   intentional, 21, 58

   marital status, 19

   unintentional, 21, 107

unlawful, 20-1, 58, 64, 85, 101, 109, 123, 158

disparate impact, 18, 57, 58, 86, 106, 107

disparate treatment, 57-8, 116

diversity initiatives, 57

DOS Visa Bulletin, 138

double time, 166

downsized organizations, 153

driving records, 35, 40

drug(s), 23, 24, 25, 47, 51, 80

   screening, 79

   test(s), 23, 24, 25, 34, 35, 36, 37, 52, 80; *see* chapter 4

   traffickers, 32

E

economic

   downturns, 115

   harm, 49

   stressful, 123

   turbulence, 153

EEO-1 form, 5

EEOC's Technical Assistance Manual (The), 24

emotional distress, 49

emotional harm, 49

employee absences, 165

employee referral program(s), 98, 105, 106, 107-08

Employee Retirement Income Security Act (ERISA), 73-4

Employer Assistance Referral Network (EARN), 104

Employment and Training Administration (ETA), 137, 140

equal employment opportunity (EEO), 6, 8, 9, 57

Equal Employment Opportunity Act, 5

Equal Employment Opportunity Commission (EEOC), 5, 7, 22, 23, 27, 57, 106, 116

Equal Pay Act, 52

essential functions, 152, 157

ethical behavior, 96, 97

E-Verify, 40-1, 146

Executive Order 11246, 9, 34, 57, 83

exempt, 55, 60, 109, 119-20, 162

exit data, 115

exit interviews, 92, 115

F

Facebook, 100

Fair and Accurate Credit Transactions (FACT) Act, 35-6

Fair Credit Reporting Act (FCRA), 23, 35, 36, 38, 39, 45, 46

Fair Labor Standards Act (FLSA), 52-3, 111, 120

Family and Medical Leave Act (FMLA), 109, 157-8

Federal Aviation Administration, 46

Federal Insurance Contributions Act (FICA), 112

Federal Motor Carrier Safety Administration, 46

Federal Railroad Administration, 46

Federal Trade Commission, 35-6, 45

Federal Transit Administration, 46

Feds Hire Vets, 127

First Amendment, 60

flexible work arrangements, 6

flexible workplaces, 76

flextime, 161

floating holiday, 166

full-time, 73, 74, 122, 138, 162

furlough, 119-20, 143

G

gap analysis, 149

Google, 100

Government Accountability Office, 37
graduation date(s), 18
group interviews, 69-70

H
H-1B, 129, 131, 132, 133, 134, 137, 141, 142, 143
H-1C, 131
H-2A, 131, 137
H-2B, 131, 134, 135, 136, 137
hiring, 10, 12, 18, 19, 21, 25, 26, 27, 28, 32, 33, 34, 38, 39, 47, 67, 70, 78, 82, 83, 87, 96, 98, 101, 104, 106, 110, 127, 137, 143, 146, 150, 151, 154; *see* chapter 6
    rehiring, 63-4
hoteling, 165
HR planning, 151
HR practice, 25
HR Talk, 40
HSPD-12 credential, 41
human capital needs, 149
human resource information system (HRIS), 7

I
I-9, 64; *see* chapter 16
identity theft, 17, 20, 36, 97
IMAGE, 146

immigrant investors, 140
Immigrant Petition for Alien Worker (Form I-140), 138, 141
intellectual property, 53
Internal Revenue Service (IRS), 73, 74, 110, 112, 114, 121
interpreter, 71

J
job
    advertisement, 96
    analysis, 67, 152, 153, 166
    applicant pools, 86
    applicants, 27, 61
    application process, 27
    bank, 55
    boards, 13, 95
    candidates, 95
    categories, 5, 116
    category, 10, 82
    characteristics, 162
    classifications, 109
    demonstration, 27
    description(s), 67, 103, 151, 152
    duties, 53 78, 113, 151, 152, 153, 157
    duty, 65
    elimination, 122
    entry-level, 20

experience, 65
fairs, 105
family, 152, 153
goals, 152
grade, 152, 153
group, 11
growth, 115
history, 68
-hopping, 68
interview, 70
level, 50, 76, 77, 106
listing(s), 55, 56
offer, 49, 71, 72,
opening(s), 101, 138
opportunities, 95, 105
opportunity, 135, 138, 139
performance, 43, 83
posting(s), 56, 85, 95
posts, 12
prospects, 86
reference immunity laws,
    30, 42
requirements, 31, 139, 151
responsibilities, 95
satisfaction, 93
security, 117
seeker(s), 13, 14, 86, 95
service offices, 11, 104
sharing, 162
temporary, 110
title(s), 52, 78, 152

vacancy announcements,
    56
vacancy notices, 27
jobless, 49
job-related, 72, 79, 82, 87
    concern, 65
    physical attributes, 82
    purpose, 26
    questions, 72
job-relatedness, 39
Jobs for Veterans Act (JVA), 9,
    55, 56, 125

K

knowledge, skills, and abilities
    (KSAs), 70, 118, 151, 152

L

Labor Condition Application or
    LCA (Form ETA 9035), 129,
    130, 131, 132, 133, 138, 142,
    143
labor pools, 8
layoffs, 10, 116, 123
leave(s), 47, 143, 157-58, 165
    FMLA, 157, 158
    paid, 51
    programs, 77
    short-term, 74
    sick, 19
libel, 30

Lilly Ledbetter Fair Pay Act, 52
lockout, 132

M

medical disability information,
18
medical examination(s), 72, 79
Medicare, 112, 114
mentoring, 105
mentors, 64
Mexico, 143-44
military
discharge papers (DD-
214), 18
discharge, 18-9
service, 19
misclassification, 114
misrepresentation, 49, 96
mode of living, 35
morale, 61, 121, 164

N

National Association of
Credential Evaluation
Services, 32
National Association of
Professional Background
Screeners (NAPBS), 39, 40
National College Credit
Recommendation Service, 32

National Labor Relations
Board, 119
national origin, 9, 17, 19, 29,
52, 57, 58, 59, 60, 62, 86,
102, 106
National Student Clearinghouse,
37
negligent referral, 30
noncompete agreements, 53, 99
nonexempt, 109, 162
nonsolicitation, 53
North American Free Trade
Agreement (NAFTA), 143-45
numeric limits, 13

O

offer letter(s), 52-4, 143
Office of Disability Employment
Policy (ODEP), 104-05
Office of Federal Contract
Compliance Programs
(OFCCP), 20, 21, 57; *see*
chapter 1
Office of Foreign Assets Control
(OFAC), 32-3
Omnibus Transportation
Employee Testing Act, 46, 80
onboard, 63
onboarding, 98; *see* chapter 11

Online Nonimmigrant Visa Electronic Application (Form DS-160), 144
on-the-job qualities, 65
on-the-job training, 112
organizational culture, 76
organizational design, 75
overtime, 66, 111, 154, 162

P

paid holidays, 166
part-time, 54, 73, 74, 117, 136, 144, 154, 161, 162
Patient Protection and Affordable Care Act, 73
pay-for-performance, 51
pension plan(s), 64, 109, 111
performance
    appraisals, 26
    considerations, 118
    criteria, 121
    documentation, 121
    evaluation, 117, 160
    issues, 121
    level, 159
    management system, 91
    problems, 120, 121
    ratings, 93
    record, 163
    review(s), 25, 26, 121, 152
    standards, 94

Permanent Employment Certification (ETA Form 9089), 136, 138
Permanent Employment of Aliens in the United States (PERM), 138
Petition for a Nonimmigrant Worker (Form I-129), 130-31, 133-34
Pipeline and Hazardous Materials Safety Administration, 46
post-hire screenings, 39
pre-employment screenings, 38, 79
Pregnancy Discrimination Act, 52
prevailing wage, 132, 137, 139
privacy, 17, 20, 26, 29, 61, 81
productivity, 68, 93, 94, 164
    metrics, 154
promissory estoppel, 49
promotion(s), 10, 59, 127, 150, 158, 160
protected class(es), 7, 10, 17, 21, 86, 102, 106

R

racial balance, 10
random generation, 13
rater bias, 26, 117

rating scales, 26

reasonable accommodations, 27, 71, 152

reasonable recruitment area, 11

Recognition of Foreign Qualifications: Professional Recognition, 31

record retention, 20, 33, 34

recruiter(s), 13, 37, 65, 66, 97, 98, 99, 102, 103; *see* chapter 10

recruitment, 10, 11, 21, 55, 97, 100, 106, 107, 108, 135, 151, 152; *see* chapter 10

reduction in force (RIF), 118, 119, 120, 122

references

    negative, 29

    personal, 38

Rehabilitation Act, 9, 80

religion, 29, 52, 57, 58, 59-60, 62, 86, 102, 106, 123

religious organizations, 60, 61

relocation costs, 49

reputation, 29, 35, 45, 62, 96, 101, 102

rescindment, 49

resume(s), 12-5, 20-2, 28, 33-4, 36, 62, 66-9, 95, 97, 104, 155

    online databases, 13

    unsolicited, 21-2

retaliation, 19, 29, 92, 158

retention, 116; *see* chapter 11

    rate(s), 39, 105, 106, 150

retirements, 89, 90

S

safety-sensitive functions, 46

security clearance, 41

seniority, 64, 117, 118, 121

SHRM Connect, 40

sick days, 19, 111

slander, 30

social media, 40, 95, 98, 105

Social Security Administration (SSA), 146

Social Security number (SSN), 17, 20, 111, 146

Social Security Number Verification Service (SSNVS), 146

Social Security, 112, 114

solution analysis, 150

special immigrants, 140

Specially Designated Nationals List (SDN List), 32

specialty occupation(s), 129, 130, 131, 133

stay interviews, 92

stress, 164

strike, 132

supervisory referrals, 26

T

talent, 78, 94, 97, 99, 101, 103, 116; *see* chapter 12
    management, 77
    poachers, 99
taxes, 114
Taxpayer Identification Number (TIN), 111
teamwork, 67, 69, 70
telecommuting, 6, 51, 158-61, 162-64
telework, 6
terminations, 90; *see* chapter 14
terrorists, 32
testing
    AIDS, 79
    alcohol, 46, 47
    genetic, 79
Title VII of the Civil Rights Act, 5, 6, 8, 10, 34, 39, 51-2, 57-8, 59-60, 83, 86, 106
TN visa, 144
training managers, 31
trend analysis, 149, 150
turnover, 20, 70, 100, 115, 121, 149, 150, 151, 164; *see* chapter 11

U

U.S. Business Leadership Network (BLN), 105
U.S. Citizenship and Immigration Services (USCIS), 41, 129, 130, 131, 132, 133, 137, 138, 139, 141, 142, 143, 146
U.S. Coast Guard, 46
U.S. Department of Defense, 80
U.S. Department of Education (DOE), 31, 37
U.S. Department of Health and Human Services, 140
U.S. Department of Homeland Security (DHS), 135, 136, 137, 145, 146
U.S. Department of Justice, 37
U.S. Department of Labor (DOL), 8, 11, 73, 104, 109, 114, 121, 122, 125, 127, 130, 131, 132, 133, 135, 136, 137, 138, 140, 142
U.S. Department of State (DOS), 137-38, 141
U.S. Department of Transportation (DOT), 46, 47
U.S. Office of Management and Budget, 140
U.S. Treasury Department, 32
undue hardship, 27, 82
Uniform Guidelines on Employee Selection

Procedures (UGESP), 19,
  58-9, 83
union contracts, 119
unionized employees, 133
unpaid interns, 113

V
validation testing methods, 59
values, 26, 114
verification of employment
  (VOE), 41-2
Veterans' Preference Advisor,
  127
veterans' preference, 18, 126-27
VETS-100 Report, 125
VETS-100A Report, 125-26
Vietnam Era Veterans'
  Readjustment Assistance Act
  (VEVRAA), 9, 55, 56, 125
vocational rehabilitation
  agencies, 104
voluntary separations, 89
volunteers, 113

W
W-4, 17, 20, 64
work authorization, 129
work/life balance, 51, 116
workforce analysis, 149
workforce composition, 154

workforce planning, 98; see
  chapter 17
Workforce Recruitment
  Program, 104
workplace bias, 60
wrongful discharge, 90, 121,
  122
workers
    contingent, 117
    priority, 139-40
    skilled, 139

Y
Yahoo!, 100

Additional
SHRM-Published Books

Business-Focused HR:
11 Processes to Drive Results
Scott P. Mondore, Shane S. Douthitt,
and Marisa A. Carson

Defining HR Success:
9 Critical Competencies for
HR Professionals
Kari R. Strobel, James N. Kurtessis,
Debra J. Cohen, and Alexander Alonso

Destination Innovation:
HR's Role in Charting the Course
Patricia M. Buhler

Employee Surveys That Work:
Improving Design, Use, and
Organizational Impact
Alec Levenson

Give Your Company a Fighting
Chance: An HR Guide to
Understanding and Preventing
Workplace Violence
Maria Greco Danaher

Got a Solution?
HR Approaches to 5 Common
and Persistent Business Problems
Dale J. Dwyer and Sheri A. Caldwell

Hidden Drivers of Success:
Leveraging Employee Insights for
Strategic Advantage
William A. Schiemann, Jerry H. Seibert,
and Brian S. Morgan

HR's Greatest Challenge:
Driving the C-Suite to
Improve Employee Engagement
and Retention
Richard P. Finnegan

The Power of Stay Interviews for
Engagement and Retention
Richard P. Finnegan

Proving the Value of HR:
How and Why to Measure ROI
Jack J. Phillips and
Patricia Pulliam Phillips

Repurposing HR:
From a Cost Center to a
Business Accelerator
Carol E.M. Anderson

Up, Down, and Sideways:
High-Impact Verbal
Communication for
HR Professionals
Patricia M. Buhler and Joel D. Worden